ICE FISHING

Guide to Great Techniques for Catching
Walleye, Pike, Perch, Trout, and Panfish

SECOND EDITION

STEVEN A. GRIFFIN

STACKPOLE
BOOKS

Essex, Connecticut
Blue Ridge Summit, Pennsylvania

STACKPOLE BOOKS

An imprint of Globe Pequot, the trade division of
The Rowman & Littlefield Publishing Group, Inc.
4501 Forbes Blvd., Ste. 200
Lanham, MD 20706
www.rowman.com
Distributed by NATIONAL BOOK NETWORK

British Library Cataloguing in Publication Information Available

Library of Congress Cataloging-in-Publication Data Available
ISBN 978-0-8117-7534-2 (paperback)
ISBN 978-0-8117-7535-9 (epub)

∞™ The paper used in this publication meets the minimum requirements of American National
Standard for Information Sciences—Permanence of Paper for Printed Library Materials, ANSI/
NISO Z39.48-1992.

As in the original edition, this book is dedicated to the people in my life—Tom J., Dale, Don, Gary, parents Howard and Margaret, grandparents May, Myrtle, and Art— who believed in the magic of ice and the fish beneath it.

And to my wife Mary Jo, who's shared and provided the magic of life; yes, our child Elizabeth has tramped plenty of snowy footprints, joined by wonderful husband Steve and amazing son Abe. Can't forget, either, fishing buddies John, Tom S., and Ken . . .

Contents

Contents

ACKNOWLEDGMENTS

Some of the material in the original *Ice Fishing: Methods & Magic,* as well as in this revised version, first appeared in slightly different form in newspapers and magazines, including the *Midland Daily News, Michigan Outdoor News, Michigan Out-of-Doors, Michigan Natural Resources,* and others.

FOREWORD

For one special year, now many years ago, I had three goals: That my wife and I would buy, rather than rent, a house. That we would expand our family. And that I would publish my first book.

Well, by the end of that year, 1985, we had a land contract on our home. Our daughter Elizabeth was a couple of months old. And *Ice Fishing: Methods and Magic* had rolled off the presses of ICS Books and, eventually, Stackpole Books.

The book did not join an extensive library. Only one other ice-fishing book was in print, and barely so. Ice-fishing magazines were scarce. Video was delivered on cassettes, long before the internet became a public information superhighway. And ice fishing itself was undergoing a metamorphosis.

Ice Fishing presented early efforts to convert boat-style electronics to winter fishing; how to build a portable shanty (since few were commercially available); and how to give up stick-and-string jigging rods in favor of spinning tackle (rods homemade, not commercially produced).

It was the end of one ice age and the beginning of another: the close of the do-it-yourself, learn-it-alone era of the hardwater sport, and the dawn of its modern iteration in which multiple technologies and industries have your back. What a great gift to have been able to experience the transition!

In time, I'd fish with one of modern ice fishing's founders, Dave Genz, chatting about ice fishing while seducing some slab-sided perch. In years to follow I'd also share ice time and/or ice talk with gurus Mark Martin, Brian "Bro" Brosdahl, Jason Mitchell, and others, each of whom would reinforce and exude what drew me to the ice long, long ago—the kid-like glee that comes from sliding a bright-colored fish onto the ice.

The glee remains, while the gear and techniques have caught up. It's time to share them—and that's this book's goal.

INTRODUCTION

It's mid-June, and I'm fumbling with a tip-up.

Sweat breaks on my forehead and yet I'm dreaming of windswept snow and numbed fingers.

Bass anglers are pulling 7-pound largemouths out of lush lake vegetation, but I'm mentally sliding a 7-inch bluegill across ice through which I've drilled a hole.

I'm not completely crazy, and I'm surely not alone.

Many anglers pursue at least part of their fishing in winter—2 million in the United States in one recent year, according to the US Fish and Wildlife Service. They averaged nineteen days on the ice apiece. For some, ice fishing is what they do when ice seals off their favorite warm-weather fishing spots. But for others, a frozen lake is their favorite fishing setting.

Yes, for some of us, summer fishing is what we do in the "off" season, when we can't ice-fish.

After all, seldom can you find faster fishing action than on a lake when it first freezes over. Never can you fry up a mess of panfish that tastes better than an ice-caught meal in midwinter. And never can you match the beauty and serenity of an ice-bound lake, any time during the long cold season.

Maybe you already know this. Perhaps we've compared notes on a frozen lake somewhere. If so, thanks for the tips you passed my way. I hope that in this book you'll find some tricks you might want to try.

Maybe, though, your ice-fishing time has been limited by a lack of information. Or a fear that you'll break through the ice or freeze solid. Or maybe you've just never taken the time to try this sport.

Regardless, come along. Whether a new ice angler or a veteran, in January or midsummer, turn a few pages. We're going ice fishing!

Fishing conditions and regulations vary as one travels across ice country. Rules change from state to province to state, even lake to lake, and sometimes season to season on the same lake. That makes it impossible for a book to provide you with all the up-to-date information you need to stay on the right side of fishing and conservation laws. And rather than do the disservice of leading you to believe otherwise, we've left the legal research to you. Get the printed regulation booklet each state's game and fish department publishes, or visit its website, or download a smartphone app to access and study up-to-date fishing regulations for the state or province in which you'll be doing your ice fishing. Watch for such restrictions as seasonal closings, bans on all or some kinds of live bait, and limits on the types of gear you can use. Note how big fish of each species must be (or sometimes, how small, too, where "slot limits" allow you to keep midsize fish) and how many you can keep. Ice shanties and on-ice use of snowmobiles, ATVs, and road-licensed vehicles are among other subjects regulated in various ways and to varying degrees in each area.

Nor do we intend to cover all the various ice-fishing strategies one can employ to take winter fish. That would require a series, not a single book. This book divides ice fishing into general subjects and species, and for each, presents basic fishing methods that work. You take it from there—adopting and then adapting the methods, if necessary, to fit the fish and conditions you face. That's part of the fun of ice fishing anyway—matching wits with your quarry.

Amid it all we'll share some sketches and essays we hope convey the special draw of the frozen lake and the fish that swim beneath the hard surface. While there are differences subtle and stunning in fishing approaches across ice country, the magic of the pursuit is shared across them all. This book's main goal is to get you on the ice with the basic know-how required to have fun and taste success.

That's when the magic will capture you.

CHAPTER 1

Ice Angler's Sunrise

SUNRISE IS IMMINENT, JUDGING BY THE RED, YELLOW, AND PURPLE clouds piled against the eastern horizon. Nearly an hour has passed since we parked the car, loaded sleds and backpacks with gear and tackle, and trudged onto this big, frozen lake.

In weeks to come, we might speed to hot spots on snowmobiles, all-terrain vehicles (ATVs), or other vehicles, but today we're satisfied walking. We checked the ice: It's 5 inches thick. We made good time walking out, step after slippery step. More than one clumsy dance move was made as horizontal ice juggled vertical anglers. Now, we're more than a mile offshore.

We're ready for some ice fishing, eager to take part in a sport that's the butt of so many jokes, cartoons, plays, and movie comedies. Some non-anglers and non–ice anglers think we're crazy, but that's OK. We were here yesterday, too, and many of the indoor jokesters would have envied our day of fresh air and the fat lake trout we carried off, two apiece.

Let's try for a replay. We'll use the same tip-ups, bait up with live smelt of about the same size. Over here's the hole through which yesterday's lunker was extracted, a lake trout of about 10 pounds. That trout shed a few drops of blood on the ice after its ascent from 100 feet down, and those stains are still visible in the snow. I'm going to set one of my tip-ups in that lucky hole.

Our other partner is already hard at work boring new holes with the power auger, glad now that he lugged it the long way out. In fifteen

An angler on a big, deep lake sets a tip-up at sunrise.

minutes he'll have drilled enough holes for a day's worth of wandering ice fishing.

You've come along to see just what this ice-fishing stuff is all about, and it's up to me and my buddy to show you why we've made all this effort.

Part of the answer is that vivid sunrise and the solitude in which we're enjoying it. We're a good half mile from our nearest angling neighbors, barely visible in the thin morning light. Spectral sunrise colors, glowing through ice shards scattered by the spinning auger, present a pleasant blend of things human, natural, and mechanical. I like, too, the crisp air that's filled our lungs and numbed our hands. You'll get used to the cold, I promise. Your fingers will be capable of fighting and icing a lake trout when the time comes.

Three of us have set a half dozen tip-ups, fewer than the maximum allowed by law here. We might add more later, but these will keep us busy enough now. At their simplest, we explained on the drive up, tip-ups are crossed sticks or platforms that suspend a reel beneath the ice and support a flag above it, connected by one of several types of spring mechanisms under tension. When a fish takes the bait and pulls on the line, the reel turns, releasing the signal flag that calls the angler to action. (There are even mechanisms that hold a rod and reel under tension, above the ice, releasing them to set the hook with a *snap!* and let the fight ensue, summer-style.)

Today our old-style tip-ups are set, and the waiting has begun. We're hoping, of course, that the lake trout will cooperate as they have on so many memorable fishing days in the past. By the time this fishing session and the ride home is over, you'll have heard about some of those days. By season's end you may hear some of the stories several times. We'll try not to exaggerate . . . too much.

This post-dawn period often seems the coldest part of the day. We pull one more time on the coat zippers, and burrow hands a little deeper into the mitts, trying to keep exposed flesh to a minimum. Cold as it is, though, I've a good hunch this is going to be a pleasant fishing day. Work is far away, and we've assembled just what we need: a car or truck to get us here, clothes that hold in most of our warmth, the auger that drilled the holes, tackle, including fishing line—a length of which is right now spinning off an underwater reel toward a fleeing lake trout!

That's your tip-up! Some groups take turns tending flags; we enjoy assigning tip-ups and tending them individually. This one's yours, the flag waving in the early morning breeze, and I swear I can see the tip-up wobbling back and forth in the hole as the fish spins off line. The water beneath us is 100 feet deep or more, and God only knows how long that flag has been flying. There's 100 yards of line on that rig, but I've seen lakers run that far and more. Let's get on over!

The fish is still swimming off as the three of us huddle over the hole in the ice, trying to decipher from the swiftly revolving reel the actions and even the mood of the trout.

Here, take the line while it's slack and wait for the trout to snug it up. First, toss those mittens aside, for this battle's to be fought barehanded. When you can feel the fish, give the line a short tug to set the hook, and then start bringing the trout in, hand-over-hand, as the fish allows you to.

This is a classic lake trout fight. For a while, it comes toward the hole fairly easily, then it's off on another stubborn run. You've always got to be ready to allow a fish, especially a big fish, to take line. It's possible to pull too hard on the line and break it. Toward the end of the fight, the fish might seem beaten, ready to be iced, but be on guard as it approaches the hole—there's almost always one more burst of angry energy before the fish slides onto the ice.

Dale is backing up behind you, gradually winding back onto the tip-up reel the line you've won from the fish. That way, the line doesn't get tangled and snarled by wind, ice chunks, and feet, unavailable if a hard-fighting fish demands it back. (If the fish runs, give Dale a yell; he'll make sure line pays freely from the tip-up.) And when the battle's over, the tip-up will be ready for quick resetting for another try at a trout.

Behind our backs the sun is rising a little higher and, with your battle with the laker nearly over, the yellow-gold rays shine on the fish's sides as it comes nearer the hole and seems to fade into view. Its mottled-gray markings almost take the breath away, so magically they appear. I'm betting you'll never get over that magic, no matter how many lakers you ice.

An angler's nerves often fray when the fish nears the hole. Carefully bring the laker to the edge of the ice, then gently start its nose upward. When things go right, it'll seem to swim up into the hole. I'll grab the trout by the gills or body, wherever I can find a handle.

I wouldn't really mind if, when trying to grab a fish of mine, you missed and knocked the fish off. But I'd sure hate to lose your first laker for you!

There, I got it! I've grabbed its gill plate and given it a hoist and toss, and there it is, flopping a few last times in the snow a few feet away.

Go ahead, spend a few minutes admiring the 8-pound trophy you've taken. If we judged you right, you'll feel a twinge of regret as the laker's blood stains the snow. Take your time; we'll start setting back up.

It may well be an hour or several before there's more action, and I sure hope you don't mind. Like most anglers, we prize the sport more than the catch. We'll try every trick we know to catch a few, and sit back and laugh if all those tricks fail. Most times, though, they don't. The next flag may come in minutes.

Your hands look like they've finally warmed after the ten-minute, barehanded, wet-line fight with the lake trout. You've retrieved the mitts you tossed aside when the battle began. And your victorious grin has mellowed into what's likely an all-day smile.

Ice fishing is funny. The sport seems so strange to those who have never tried it, so natural to those of us who love it. And believe me, it's possible to learn quickly to love it.

Dale Smith, who became a longtime fishing partner and friend, first converted me into a committed ice angler. I'd dabbled, but this would be different. Dale and I had spent some mid-November deer-hunting time together, and one day we went scouting for new hunting grounds, pulling into a state forest campground adjacent to a large piece of state-owned land. Through the camp flowed a creek, backed up by a dam on a large river several miles downstream. Thus impounded, the creek had virtually no current, and it froze early. Yes, on this late-fall day, the creek was frozen, and that short-circuited all our deer-hunting ideas

At the sight of the frozen backwaters, Dale put all his other plans on the back burner. In an instant he had thrown a large rock onto the ice and, when it didn't even produce a crunch, he grabbed the spud that rode in the back of his car from fall through spring. Tapping carefully for signs of weakness in the ice, he roamed out from shore, finally punching a hole a few feet out. The ice was safe—several inches thick.

We hustled back to town, where Dale collected a couple of short, light fishing rods and a handful of tiny jigging lures composed of painted chunks of metal on small single hooks. At a nearby sporting goods store, we bought a couple of dozen little grubs called wax worms for bait. Summer-fishing fans, too, we already had our fishing licenses. In less than an hour, we were back on the frozen creek.

Dale was, anyway. I was, shall we say, tentative. He snuck out, cut a hole in the ice, and, minutes later—while high-power deer rifles boomed in the distance and shoppers elsewhere examined Thanksgiving turkeys—he pulled a chunky bluegill onto the ice. Then another. After four or five nice 'gills flopped onto the ice, Dale urged me again to join him. I grabbed a jigging rod and all the courage I could muster and stepped out from shore, walking carefully along the path Dale had taken. He quickly showed me how to set the tiny bobber to hold the lure just off bottom in the 4-foot-deep water, how to jiggle the rod lightly and detect a strike when the bobber wiggled or dove, and, finally, how to ice a bluegill once it struck. More even than the bluegill, I was hooked!

All the way home that day, and for many weeks afterward, I bombarded Dale with questions. I wanted to learn all I could about ice fishing, and the sooner the better. Dale patiently fielded my many questions. Usually his answers were simpler than the inquiries. And maybe that's what I like best about ice fishing. It's a straightforward sport. You can get just as fancy with your fishing gear as you like, but ice fishing remains a relatively simple game.

You can count on motorized vehicles on the ice to take you to your fishing spot, but walking's often easier and safer. You can yank to life a gas-powered auger or squeeze the trigger on an electric one and guide it quickly through a foot of ice or more, but a $25 spud or $75 hand auger will do the same job, even if it takes a little more work and time. You can assemble a fancy collection of tackle, but everything you really need will fit in a five-gallon plastic bucket, and you won't need to have $100 invested.

You do, however, need the desire to head onto the ice in the first place.

Back in college, tuition, books, and less-academic expenditures had deflated our budgets, and my roommate and I had grown weary of macaroni and cheese and spaghetti. We heard that large perch were biting well through the ice of a small lake nearby, and our imaginations cooked up a mess of perch fillets bubbling in hot grease. Neither of us had ice-fishing experience, but we had vivid imaginations and plenty of self-confidence.

It turned out that the report was actually reversed: They were actually *small perch* in a *large lake*.

Nonetheless, we threaded newly purchased lines and lures down holes left over by previous anglers, easing the hooks down into about 20 feet of water beneath the foot-thick ice. The perch, mostly 6-inchers and even smaller, inhaled the grub-baited lures as soon as they fell. After two hours, a dozen line tangles, and even an early-spring rain, we'd filled a small bucket with perch.

Cleaning the catch was the next chore, and fellow dormitory residents grumbled about our fish-filleting in the shared kitchen. They had thought of ice fishing as crazy and now viewed our sopping-wet, fish-cleaning reappearance as proof. But those tiny fillets, rolled in pancake flour and fried in hot oil, produced one of the most memorable meals of my life. We'd been ice fishing—but I wasn't yet an ice fisher. Dale would change that, and I'd eventually draw others into the fold.

My wife Mary Jo and I were married for three full years before she saw Higgins Lake, consistently rated one of Michigan's most beautiful lakes, when it was unfrozen. Higgins is a big lake, plenty deep once you've ranged far enough offshore to where a drop-off falls about 40 feet down in 40 feet of walking. A similar drop farther out breaks into more than 100 feet of water. Along those ledges roam lake trout and splake, the latter an interesting hybrid cross of lake and brook trout.

We'd coaxed Mary Jo into joining us on Higgins Lake this winter day. We'd been taking trout with some regularity but never in what you'd call red-hot action. Three friends joined us as we walked out to the drop-off and finally over 110 feet of water. We'd built snow castles the previous day to mark the best holes and kill some of the hours in which even the good holes didn't pay off.

We scattered to those holes and started setting tip-ups. "How deep is it here?" asked a friend who'd not fished this lake before. I told him a little more 100 feet. "But I have 150 feet of line out," he protested, "and still haven't hit bottom."

A light went on in his head and his face broke into a rather foolish smile as he set the hook and fought a hungry trout toward the surface. The splake, eager for a meal, hadn't even waited for the minnow to reach bottom before engulfing it and swimming off.

Fred fought his fish while the rest of us laughed at the fast action. And before his fish came through the hole, another flag was flying. Then another. For two hours the fish kept us busy chasing flags, fighting fish, and rebaiting. When we finally called it a day, we were a single fish short of the limit for all five anglers. And Mary Jo had a new appreciation for one of Michigan's most beautiful lakes—frozen or unfrozen.

Not many ice-fishing outings produce that kind of action. But similar experiences are relived on a thousand other outings in ice country, with new memories born each winter.

Some fishing excursions are memorable for reasons other than the number of fish caught. One of my most enjoyable ice-fishing trips came on a Christmas Day. As a family gathering stretched into the hours and the outdoor temperature climbed into the 30s, Mary Jo, bless her, leaned over and whispered into my ear, "Let's go ice fishing!"

In ten minutes I'd traded tie and dress shoes for wool scarf and felt-pac boots. The van already held my fishing tackle, as it seems to do all winter. We were quickly bound for an impoundment nearby.

The lake was all but deserted, most of its frequent anglers no doubt held ashore by domestic matters and perhaps spouses less understanding than mine.

A couple of hours later, when a kid with a brand-new pair of Christmas ice skates bladed over to check us out, we showed him our dozen crappies and bluegills, plus a 25-inch pike we were about to release. We'd just wanted a few panfish for dinner and a few hours alone in the outdoors. We'd succeeded on both counts.

For either peace or productive fishing, I'll take ice-time anytime. Usually I find both.

I'm pretty sure I catch more fish per hour ice fishing than in open water. Most ice anglers with whom I've compared notes agree. There are plenty of reasons offered for the better success rate of ice anglers, although many of them are untested.

I think we focus better on our fishing when the weather's cold and the water's hard. You can easily doze off in a boat gently bobbing on a summer lake. But in the winter all of nature's forces direct your attention to your fishing line, and maybe the electronic devices that have developed to enrich the sport.

The colder it gets, the harder you stare at that fishing hole, the line you've threaded down through it, and the information displayed on your electronic fish-finder or underwater camera. And the more attention you pay to your fishing, the more success you can expect.

Fish are a bit more predictable in winter than in warm-weather months, too. Perhaps it's because they aren't as active. They are cold-blooded creatures, so when the water temperature drops, so does their metabolism and body activity. They don't burn up as much energy so they don't need to eat as much. But there isn't as much natural food available to them as in summer either, now that the major food-producing segment of the lake is closed for the winter. So, your offering faces less competition. And since weed growth slows until the vegetation eventually dies back in winter, the fish can even see your bait more easily. Declining dissolved oxygen content, as those decaying weeds consume rather than produce oxygen, concentrates fish where more oxygen remains, too.

In summer, frequent changes in weather, lake-top activity, or other factors can make it impossible to enjoy similar fishing success on two consecutive days. But in winter, if you caught fish from a certain hole in the ice on a certain bait yesterday, you'd best copy your tactics today.

Fish don't seem quite as spooky under the ice as they do when those same waters are open. Maybe the impact of sunlight is reduced when that light is filtered through several inches of ice and snow.

That roof over the lake probably cuts the noise, too. Even though snowmobiles, ATVs, or even cars and trucks rumbling by may disrupt your fishing momentarily, it's still a smaller problem than a summer lake chock-full of ski and wakeboard boats.

The fish you catch in winter will likely taste better than those you caught from the same lake last summer. Mine do, anyway. Maybe it's because of the extra effort involved in catching them through the ice. Or perhaps there's some biological reason involving changes in the fish's diet or activity level. The superb taste of winter fish likely reflects the cold water, cold air, and snow that, together, keep spoilage to a minimum. Experts say a fish begins to deteriorate as soon as it dies. Cold, however, slows that spoilage greatly.

The lake trout you caught at the beginning of this chapter will convince you of the fine eating qualities of ice-caught fish, I'm certain. Keep it cold and fillet it out as soon as you get home. Cut the orange-ish fillets crossways into "fingers," roll them in batter (as simple as pancake flour; I like to add cornmeal, 50–50), and pop the strips into hot oil for a few minutes on each side. Those chunks of gourmet fare will make strong argument for a long ice-fishing career. Their flavor challenges, but never overshadows, the magic of walking upon frozen water, the mystery of

Mary Jo Griffin, the author's wife, releases a northern pike caught on a Christmas Day outing.

catching fish big and small far below you, and the charm of hours spent with kindred souls.

We have a lot in common, after all. Even though you're new to the ice and we spend much of the winter upon it, we all jumped with the same alarm when the ice boomed. It was just more safe ice forming, though, not too-thin ice giving way to too-heavy anglers.

We've shared the launching of a winter day. Winter clouds often hang brilliant white against a deep-blue sky, and even leaden-gray skies promise excitement in new snow on the way. When the waters freeze we share domain over every lake. We don't need boats or fancy gear—just an access point from which we can walk onto the frozen waters.

Come again to this lake, or to any of thousands that freeze across the northern United States and Canada each winter. You'll get cold, tired, and, once in awhile, maybe even a little bit bored. But when that little bobber twitches, the spring strike indicator dips, or the tip-up flag flies, your heart will beat with renewed vigor.

And after a season or two, your spirits will rise nearly as high just *remembering* a good ice-fishing day. You'll look forward to winter when, heavily clothed and in the company of some good friends, you'll savor again an ice angler's sunrise.

Chapter 2

Safety

Often I've chatted with veteran ice anglers, swapping insights and stories on catches, baits, and the weather, when the conversation shifted to danger: times they'd dropped through the ice, emerging soaked-through but thankfully quite alive.

Maybe they were walking over water only a few feet deep. Perhaps the water was deeper, but they were able to use something—handheld rescue spikes, a spud, a knife, a rope thrown by a quick-thinking buddy—to pull themselves onto the ice. Maybe they were just plain lucky and bobbed back to the surface, kicked their feet, and were out.

The next season, the next day, or maybe even yet the same day, they were back on the ice, a little more cautious but no less enthusiastic about their sport.

I know of other people, however, who fell through the ice and just barely got themselves out. They quickly swore they'd never again trust a frozen body of water to support them. Some won't even walk on a skating rink, even though they know there's concrete, not water, beneath its ice!

Even those folks, however, are among the lucky ones.

During any winter in ice country, local news tells of people who plunged through the ice. Not all were anglers on foot. Some were on snowmobiles, either for fishing transportation or recreation on its own merits. Some were on all-terrain vehicles, and others yet traversing frozen lakes or streams in cars or trucks. Some were kids at play.

The people in these stories, however they came to be on the ice, had one thing in common: They died. Divers had to pull their bodies from

An angler checks the thickness and quality of a lake's ice with a spud. Its sharp edge will punch through the ice before the person does.

lakes upon which they should have had fun. Their families and friends became survivors, bereaved, when they should have shared many more years with those who drowned or died of exposure.

I noticed a crowd at one end of a Michigan lake one Saturday morning in February, and ambled over to where divers from the local sheriff's department were clamping heavy cables onto a mostly submerged snowmobile, while a wrecker crew stood ready to drag the sled ashore. Nobody seemed eager to talk about what had happened to the snowmobile's riders.

Later I found that a husband and wife had been on this machine the previous night. New to the lake, they didn't know that it was connected by an open channel to another small lake, and into that channel they had driven. A bystander heard the yelling and quickly rescued the driver, but his wife was in the water for forty minutes before a rescue squad pulled her out. She was rushed to a hospital, where she was lying while I was watching workers pull the snowmobile from the icy waters. She lay in the hospital for several days before she died.

That same weekend, elsewhere in the state, an ice angler died when the pickup truck he was driving plunged through the ice over a Great Lakes bay. A kid, ice-skating, drowned after breaking through thin ice.

Every year people die after falling through ice. In almost every case, one or more violations of basic safety precautions can be pinpointed as contributing to the tragedy. Ice safety rules are similar to those for driving a car or truck. You can bend the rules, even break them outright, and get away with it—some or even most times. But no matter how often or how seldom you break those rules, there's a chance that when you do, you're going to get caught. And on the ice, just as in a car, the penalty for breaking the rules might be your life.

The first rule of ice safety is respect. Ice is not a living creature, of course, but it often resembles one. It's born and then builds strength through its early life. Occasional illnesses may reduce that strength, and eventually, it's going to weaken and, finally, pass away. You have to monitor its health, keeping an eye alert for changes, indications that it's unsafe, and temper every decision with the knowledge that the water beneath the ice can easily and quickly take your life.

You must be responsible for your own actions.

Whether you choose to ice-fish or pursue another sport on a frozen lake is your decision. Once made, it's you who must guard your own safety.

There have been many basic rules listed through the years on just what constitutes safe ice. These list ice thicknesses in inches, matching those measurements to activities considered safe. They're good guidelines, generally, but that's all. Too many other variables directly and emphatically affect ice safety. Few agencies issue specific guidelines anymore.

I once had a lengthy chat with Eric Olsen, a marine education specialist in the Michigan Department of Natural Resources. A year-round water and boat safety expert, he had a special interest in ice safety, having spent countless hours on frozen waters for both work and recreation. He explained the challenges of setting firm ice-safety rules to cover all situations. "While 3 inches of ice on a farm pond may hold a person with little danger, that same 3 inches on a moving stream or a lake with springs, stumps, marine growth, and currents could be very dangerous. On the Great Lakes, one step from 3-foot ice, you may find a lead with nothing more than skim ice and a little snow," the result of sub-bodies of water freezing at differing rates.

Yes, conditions vary, and it's the job of an ice angler to keep track of them.

The first piece of ice-fishing equipment I recommend is a spud, a heavy tool that most resembles a long-handled chisel. Store salesclerks tell you spuds are for chipping holes in the ice, and they do work well for that. But they've a far more important role as tools to test the thickness and quality of the ice.

Whenever there's the least shadow of a doubt about the thickness of a lake's ice—and that's most of the time—I walk very slowly, thudding the ice soundly with a spud on each step or two. I've been laughed at for being cautious on ice that proved to be firm and a foot thick, but more than once my jaw has dropped when one good *thunk* poked right through. That obviously meant there was far too little ice for me to be walking upon, and I quickly backstepped to shore to wait for another batch of cold weather to firm up the footing. Otherwise, when you've reached your fishing spot, some quick work with the spud or an auger—manual or power—will quickly further prove the ice's quality and thickness, and soon you're fishing.

(This isn't exactly a safety matter, but make sure your spud has a wrist strap so that when testing ice or spudding a hole, you can't let the big chisel slip through your hands when the last thud surprises you when it suddenly pokes through the ice. Many spuds lie on lake bottoms.)

Don't chop or bore test holes in the path on which other anglers will walk. My only ice-fishing dunking came one day when I took my wife to a popular fishing spot where I had been catching bluegills and crappies for a couple of weeks. I knew the ice was more than 6 inches thick. As I had on many previous days, I stepped off the end of a dock at water's edge—only this time I kept right on going, clear up to my waist. I turned to see the half-angry, half-amused face of my wife. "How can I help you?"

she asked, and I mumbled something ambiguous as I pulled myself back onto the dock.

Someone had decided to chop their test hole at the end of the dock, and I'd stepped squarely into it. The fishing trip, along with my comfort and composure, was shot because of that—and because I'd been too excited about fishing to look carefully at the ice there.

Remember always that ice quality varies greatly from lake to lake, season to season, even day to day. It can be the good clear blue or black ice that signals strength, or it can look porous, milky, spongy, rotten, or honeycombed. Stay onshore unless you're certain the ice is safe. And don't ever assume that an entire lake is covered with the same quality or thickness of ice. More than once I've cut a hole in the ice 10 inches thick, later moving a few dozen yards away to discover the ice there just 3 inches thick. That was still enough for my walk-on fishing, but to a snowmobiler or on-ice car driver, it could have meant disaster.

Variations are especially common along shore, where ice is often thin to start with and quick to deteriorate when water levels change, sun starts the melt-down process, or runoff water begins cutting it. Deadheads, docks, posts, and stream inlets and outlets spell trouble, too. Moving water and warmth cut ice. Dark objects warm in the sun and soften or melt ice and create a danger zone. Be especially careful if you're going to fish on an impoundment; a lake formed by a dammed river always has water movement within it. So do spring-fed lakes; often, they'll have patches of thin ice all winter. So ask around about spots known to remain iffy.

New ice is generally much stronger than old; a couple of inches of new, clear ice may be strong enough to support you while even a foot or more of old, air-bubbled ice may not. But no matter what kind of lake or impoundment, the season's first ice can be inconsistent. And if a few inches of insulating snow blankets an inch or two of hard new ice, that will dramatically slow the formation of more.

There was a time when state agencies and other authorities—and even an earlier version of this book—offered detailed guidelines to how thick ice should be for safe fishing and travel. Almost always, they added a "your results may vary" note: The quality of ice, its age, your size, and the heft of the vehicle you use all made measurement guides imprecise. Now, most of them offer advice similar to this, lightly paraphrased, from Michigan's Department of Natural Resources:

- Your safety is your responsibility!
- There is no reliable "inch-thickness" guide to determine if ice is safe.
- You can and should test ice thickness and quality using a spud, needle bar, or auger.
- The strongest ice is clear with a bluish tint.
- Ice that appears milky is likely weak, formed by melted and refrozen snow.
- Stay off slush-topped ice. Even when it finally freezes, once-slush ice is only half as strong as clear ice, a result of its freezing from the top and not the bottom.
- A sudden cold front with low temperatures can within a half day create cracks that can pose step-in dangers or become covered and hidden beneath thin ice or snow.
- A warm spell may take several days to weaken ice, with ice thawing during the day and refreezing at night. This refrozen ice is not as firm as when first formed.
- Ice weakens with age.
- Be extra cautious if there's water around the shoreline of an ice-topped lake.
- Many lakes have currents within them; the stronger the lake's current, the more likely its ice will erode.
- Avoid areas of ice with protruding debris such as logs or brush.
- Keep an eye out for dock bubblers or de-icers. If they do their job, they imperil your ice-fishing safety.

The New Hampshire Fish and Game Department cited advice from the US Army Cold Regions Research and Engineering Laboratory there: "There should be a minimum of 6 inches of hard ice before individual foot travel, and 8–10 inches of hard ice for snow machine or off-highway recreational vehicle travel." Those guidelines are more conservative than most anglers follow, but they'll keep you out of trouble, as will the state agency's advice: "It is never advisable to drive vehicles onto the ice."

People do drive cars and trucks on ice every winter, of course, and most of them never experience a problem. Some fisheries, such as that on the massive Lake of the Woods (we'll talk about it later), are built upon truck travel. But I still believe the only lake absolutely safe for car or truck travel is one frozen completely to the bottom.

If you must drive on the ice, at least keep the windows down and the doors ajar. If your car breaks through and the windows and doors are tight or their motors or switches short-circuit, you might not be able to get out of the vehicle. Seat belts are great when you're driving on a road, but you might consider keeping them unbuckled when on the ice, since they'd make escape just that much slower.

In shallow water this truck's plunge poses a combination of inconvenience and embarrassment; in deeper water it could have brought disaster.

No matter how I'm moving across the ice—on foot, on a snowmobile, or in a car—I try to tell myself two things every time I go ice fishing:

- Sooner or later, I'm going to break through, so I remain prepared to self-rescue.
- By being cautious, I can substantially lessen the odds that it's going to happen on this particular day.

Think ahead. Realize that you can indeed break through the ice. You might wear a personal flotation device (life jacket) or an ice-fishing suit into which flotation material has been incorporated (it's not US Coast Guard–approved like a life jacket, but it is a potential lifesaver if you drop in). Remember, too, that almost any cold-weather clothing you wear will trap air and keep you afloat long enough for rescue by yourself or others.

Eric Olsen, my Michigan DNR ice-safety friend, added long-ago advice that still holds:

- If you do go through the ice, try to stay on top of the water.
- Don't panic: Remember, your clothes will hold air and help you float for awhile.
- Get out any way you can. You may have to float on your back and work your way out by kicking your feet, in effect swimming out of danger.
- If you can, get your upper body up on the ice and use whatever handholds you can to roll out of the water. [Each of my ice-fishing coats has a set of spikes in its upper right-hand pocket. Without searching or even looking, I can extract them in seconds and drive their sharp points into the ice for enough bite to pull myself out of the water. Some of the best new ice-fishing coats have holders for spikes; some even come equipped with them.]
- Once atop the ice, stay spread out, and squirm, crawl, or roll to safety. Make and execute your self-rescue decision fast. It won't be long before you start feeling the ill effects of hypothermia.

- When you get out and are on safe ice, get to warmth and safety as quickly as possible. If you are alone and headed for a car started mechanically by a key, get your car keys out as soon as you leave the water. That may be impossible in a minute or two, after your pockets freeze solid.

- In most cases the path you took to the hole is the safest one away from it. Roll away from the hole until you can safely stand up. Your clothes will quickly freeze, so get moving toward safety.

(I plunged through thin ice on a Nebraska lake one November day trying to recover a deer I had shot. The water was chest deep, and I was able to climb atop the ice—but it broke, again and again. By the time I finally reached the shore, my hands were quickly becoming too cold to be of use, and I could tell that my thinking was getting fuzzy. I pointed myself to the trail to my car, about a mile away, and began trudging through the brisk wind and 15°F temps. With the help of a rancher who thought I might need assistance with the deer and so was headed my way, I made it. But it was my closest call ever, and one I don't want to repeat.)

Maybe you're not the one who fell through, but someone near you has. Experts say first make sure you don't do anything to place yourself in the same jeopardy, breaking through the ice yourself and thus creating another victim. Use a ladder, tree limb, article of clothing, rope, or anything else you can find to reach out and assist them. If you have to go on the ice, spread your weight as much as possible.

Boaters often carry a throw rope, a floating line within a soft nylon bag that becomes a projectile from which the line pays out in flight. The bitter (loose) end of the line is tied in a loop that fits over your non-throwing hand. Make a soft underhand toss to or, better yet, beyond the victim. If you miss, you can bring the line in and recoil the line for a second toss, like a conventional rope. You might pack the bag with snow or water for a long heave. If they can, have the victim tie the line around them before their hands get too cold to do it or even hold on. Taking a tip from my boater friends: I carry a marine throw bag in my ice gear. Its few ounces of heft would be well worth it if needed. It's a constant and subtle reminder, too, that safety should be a constant concern.

Experts once spoke of the "mammalian diving reflex," in which a cold-water-immersed person's body would concentrate warmth in the areas most important for survival. Even a person who seemed beyond help (dead) could sometimes be saved, thanks to this automatic reflex.

Lifesaving has evolved, and newer science describes four phases of cold-water drowning, the first an automatic "gasp" reflex that occurs in response to the skin cooling rapidly. (How rapidly? Some say water speeds cooling four-fold over the same temperature in air.) If the head's underwater, that gasp inhales water that can fill the lungs, causing drowning. That's where it's so important that a life jacket, float coat, or even just your air-holding outerwear can give you some buoyancy. You may also hyperventilate, or breathe too quickly. Try to evade the panic and control your breathing.

All that's in the first minute in the water. After five to fifteen minutes, your body tries to preserve its core heat by decreasing blood flow to the extremities, which are of little use now in keeping you afloat.

Next is hypothermia—thirty minutes or more in for most adults. Try to fight off panic. Symptoms include shivering, slow and shallow breathing, confusion, fatigue or drowsiness, slurred speech, loss of coordination, and/or weak pulse.

The danger doesn't end at rescue. Once hypothermia sets in, "circumrescue collapse," apparently related to blood pressure failure, can take place before, during, or after rescue and requires professional medical attention.

(Want to learn more about cold-water dangers and responses? The National Center for Cold Water Safety, coldwatersafety.org, has great information.)

None of that sounds like much fun, does it? Rescue and first-aid tips could save a life, but it's so much better to use the respect and judgment required to avoid such emergencies.

Whatever you do, don't trust someone else's judgment. I sat on a large lake one day, on good ice nearly 3 inches thick, my personal practical minimum for widely scattered anglers on foot. I fished awhile, looked up, and watched a snowmobile zooming across that lake, several hundred yards farther out from shore. I know that had the driver stopped the machine, or had it stalled, machine and driver would have plunged through the ice. And I'm not sure that the ice would have been thick enough to allow me to go to the driver's rescue.

It was a great reminder not to rush to a fishing spot just because others or their vehicles are already there. I'd rather be the foolish-looking angler who carefully taps the ice with a spud, sneaking ever so cautiously onto the ice, only to find with the first test hole that there's a solid 18 inches of ice.

Ice, properly respected, is a platform on which you can build many enjoyable fishing experiences.

Play it safe, and then laugh at how safe you're playing it. That leaves you free, after all, to relax and enjoy the remainder of the outing.

CHAPTER 3

First Ice

THE CALENDAR REALLY ISN'T KIND TO THE ICE ANGLER. GROUSE SEASON opens on a certain date, pheasant season on another. You can find the opening day of the deer or stream-trout season on a calendar. But ice-fishing season doesn't open until Mother Nature says so.

So, fans of the ice begin watching puddles in November, hoping that ever-colder mornings create a skim of ice. I watch the dog's outdoor water dish. Only when it refreezes each night can I rationally begin digging out tip-ups, jigging poles, and augers. And still we must wait a few weeks until small lakes, then larger bodies of water, freeze over solidly enough to support our fishing efforts.

We've emphasized safety already. Don't go on a lake you're unsure of. But some things are certain, among them the fact that as soon as it's safe to get on the ice, the fish will be there.

I once asked a fish biologist why early-season first-ice fishing is so much more productive than any other fishing of the season. He explained that winter's approach brings a cooling down of water, a shutdown in the lake's food factory, and a decline, too, in the metabolism of fish and their need for food. But those things don't happen all at once. Those changes really begin in fall, when less sunlight reaches the water each day and air and water temperatures begin to drop. Smaller organisms and plants seem to feel the changes first, reproducing and growing more slowly, if at all. That leaves panfish and gamefish in the midst of pre-winter feeding, even as food supplies become scarcer. When winter deepens, panfish and larger predator fish, all cold-blooded creatures, will trim their activity

When safe ice forms, anglers quickly gather for some of the season's finest fishing.

levels to match the cooler conditions in which they live. But beneath this early ice, they're active.

So tip-ups fly often for ice fishers working first ice for northern pike and walleyes. Crappies and bluegills often keep a panfish angler so busy, one can only keep up with the action of one rod, even though most states allow us to fish with more. The first few weeks of safe ice are when an ice angler is most apt to catch largemouth bass. We once even iced a 7-pound, early-ice carp that grabbed a teardrop-and-wax-worm combination intended to catch bluegills. You never know what's going to happen on the season's first ice, but it's almost guaranteed to be memorable.

Near my mid-central Michigan home, we've ice-fished, tentatively and admittedly seldom, just a few days after Thanksgiving when winter arrived early. Usually, but not always, we've been on safe ice by Christmas Day. Sometimes, sadly, it's been mid-January. But whenever it arrives, the start of the ice-fishing season is something not to be missed.

I prepare well in advance. Late summer sometimes. It used to be that the first ice outing would find me on the ice mumbling—auger or spud dull, tip-ups tangled up, jigging rods wrapped with aged and abused line, tied to rusted lures. No longer does first ice find me unprepared, and probably for at least two reasons. One, I've discovered that an hour's work in the basement can save a day's troubles on the ice, and I certainly don't want to compromise the best fishing of the season. Two, I now get so excited about the coming ice fishing that, long before ice arrives, I've generally dug out and fixed up the tackle—just for the preseason satisfaction of it.

You don't need much in the way of equipment for early-season fishing. Since ice hasn't yet thickened much, a spud is handier than an auger, and a good safety precaution as well. You must assume that early ice is never safe. Use the spud to whack the ice in front of you as you proceed onto the lake. Cutting a test hole to check the ice's thickness is a good idea, too; just don't do it where other anglers are likely to be walking.

You probably won't have to venture far onto a lake now to sample its action. Crappies and bluegills are often in water less than 10 feet deep, and those depths are often good for pike and walleyes as well.

A northern pike on the season's first fishable ice

The simplest early-season fishing is for panfish. This time of the year crappies and bluegills seem to form large, mixed schools, and the first-ice action they provide can be frantic. But pike, walleye, and perch fishing can be splendid, too.

The fishing is easily worth the minimal effort required to watch those driveway puddles as they begin to harden in fall, worth the gas to double-check on your favorite lake even before you think ice could have formed.

For there's no opening day for ice fishing. Someone will always get on the lake before you. Let them. Make sure the ice is safe before you risk your life for a bucket of fish.

But make sure, too, that when the conditions are safe, you're there and fishing.

The calendar may be unkind to the ice fisher, but Mother Nature is generous with her fish when the ice season finally opens.

CHAPTER 4

Stay Warm

To enjoy fishing on the ice, you must first learn to respect and minimize the chances of your falling through it. Then, you need to maintain your own warmth. If you don't stay warm, you'll become either a miserable ice angler or a former ice angler. A comfortable angler is best prepared to pay close attention to their fishing, too.

Modern suits and boots, and cozy shelters such as this insulated flip-over tent, make ice fishing a cozy adventure.

Fortunately, more good cold-weather clothing is now available, across a wide price range, than ever before.

Time was, an ice angler assembled their clothing and footwear the same way they gathered most of the rest of their gear: by figuring out how to use for ice fishing something designed for some other purpose. Sometimes that meant wearing cold-weather work clothing, heavyweight insulated cotton duck outerwear made by Carhartt and other manufacturers, as appreciated on the ice as on the job site for which it was designed. Plenty of ice anglers still spend comfortable winters in insulated cotton duck suits.

The Korean War in the 1950s left a legacy of military surplus cold-weather clothing, joining even older surplus gear already on the ice. My first pair of ice-fishing pants were leather with fleece lining—part of an Air Force flight suit for duty in unheated fighters and bombers, the surplus store clerk said. They were heavy and cumbersome, but my, were they warm! One of my buddies did all of his ice fishing in Navy deck pants, corduroy with blanket-wool lining. He stayed warm, too.

More commonly, many a civilian red-and-black-plaid woolen deer hunting suit hit the ice after deer season.

Snowmobiling brought the one-piece or bibs-and-jacket nylon suits that made staying warm simpler and more affordable, whether on a snowmachine or pulling an ice sled.

And then finally, about the time portable, nylon-topped ice-fishing shanties came along to provide shelter against wind and cold, clever tailors began designing suits from the same robust material. Their triumph? The ice-fishing suit! Typically a parka or jacket over a pair of bibs, an ice suit allows you to literally wear your shanty, moving around easily and comfortably while traveling to and from your shelter, if using one, and while open-air ice fishing. They're made by several manufacturers, among them Striker, StrikeMaster, Eskimo, Ice Armor (Clam), Ice Runner, and Simms.

The ice suit's exterior is your tent, and like that structure, you want it windproof, waterproof, and breathable. Look for the garment's Durable Water Repellency (DWR) rating to determine how well it fends off water. The higher the rating, the better. Sealed seams keep sewing holes and thread from wicking in rain and melting snow. Drawstrings at waist or jacket hem keep chills out. And breathability—the uncanny ability of special fabrics to keep water out while letting moist air escape—helps avoid overheating.

Inside, insulation comes in a variety of brands and types—many based on PrimaLoft or other proprietary synthetics. Fleece lining in some suits adds comfort.

Reflective material incorporated in many designs adds safety: You can be spotted at night by a speeding snowmobile, for example, or by a rescuer casting a flashlight beam across the ice. In the bibs, knee and seat padding provide comfort in those key places. Jumping onto the latest deer-hunting trend, some makers have incorporated battery-powered heating elements in the back and hip areas of their ice garments, including float suits.

Stepping up a notch on safety, you can select an ice suit into which buoyant closed-cell polyurethane insulation has been incorporated. Don't mistake a float coat for a life jacket; the suits haven't been US Coast Guard certified. But one will keep you afloat up to a couple of hours after falling through the ice, and that's especially important early and late in the season, when conditions are diciest, and on waterways where fractures and other events create hazards.

A conventional hunting suit, particularly one in which there's a wearable liner within the parka, makes a good ice-fishing outfit. You can wear the outer coat and liner, or just one or the other, to match the conditions and your activity level. That's especially handy if you're doing some of your fishing in a shelter, such as a hard-walled shanty or portable shelter or tent, and some outdoors, such as tending tip-ups.

Using What You've Got

Not ready to take the $500-plus plunge for a dedicated ice-fishing suit, or the biggest chunk of that for a hunting suit? You can still enjoy this great sport. Head for the winter clothes closet; you'll likely find something there that will serve.

Got a heavy red-and-black-plaid deer-hunting suit? Remember that for decades, an ice angler's first choice in cold-weather clothing material was simple: wool. Long underwear, shirt-jackets, and outerwear all were of wool, and for good reason. This natural material is an excellent insulator and, importantly, retains much of its insulating value when wet. An ice angler clad in wool could—and can—venture out in practically any weather, even rain or snow, and put in a full fishing day without chill. Compared to modern materials, wool is heavy when dry and heavier when wet, but it remains a solid choice for outdoor activities including ice fishing.

Ice anglers and other winter recreationists a few decades ago often wore goose down–filled clothing, some of it military surplus. It provided good insulation and was comparatively lightweight yet bulky, but practically no good at all when wet. Still, I cherish a knee-length parka jammed with prime goose down within a water-repellent exterior and topped with a fur-ruffed hood; it's my go-to when the thermometer heads below 0°F—when dry cold, not moisture, is the challenge.

Modern fills are nearly as warm as dry down and offer real advantages over it, tops among them that they retain much of their air-trapping insulating properties if they become wet. Synthetic materials wash up more easily, dry quicker, and are in many cases cheaper than those filled with down.

Yes, there are still places for heirloom woolen and down-filled clothing in today's ice-fishing wardrobe, in which even better wools and high-quality down are available. Still, for many anglers there's no better clothing material, exterior and fill alike, than synthetics.

Thank the snowmobile for those innovations. When the tracked machines became super popular in the 1960s and 1970s, people buying and riding power sleds clamored for clothing that would keep them warm. Responding to that demand, the cold-weather clothing industry made available one-piece, synthetic-filled, nylon-shelled jumpsuits. These suits were wind resistant, hooded, and built to last. Pretty affordable, too. Many of them are still in use today. Joining them on the rack were jacket and bib overall or coat-and-pant sets. Many are still in use, and they still keep their owners warm.

Be it cutting-edge, classic, or vintage, I'm a fan of the two-piece suit, ideally bibbed overalls with a heavy coat or parka. That provides the flexibility of leaving the coat open if the day is warm, closing it tightly if it's cold, or removing it entirely if working hard spudding a hole or enjoying an unusually nice springtime ice-fishing outing.

Ice-fishing outerwear seems costly, but think of it as an investment in many years of long seasons of fun and comfort—and, depending on your choice, safety. Where we once used clothing from hunting and other sports for ice fishing, now we often find ourselves grabbing the ice-fishing duds when it's time to watch a snowmobile race, blow snow from the driveway, or fish from a cold-weather boat or pier. I've even worn my ice suit sledding with my grandson on a cold winter day—you hardly need the sled!

Whatever assortment of clothing you assemble, make sure at least one piece has a heavy hood. You'll almost certainly be wearing a stocking cap or hat with ear flaps, but when the winds begin to whip across a frozen lake, the hood adds immeasurable comfort atop the hat. And whether or not the hood is on your head, it guards the back of your neck against those cold winds.

When trying on outerwear you plan to wear ice fishing, make sure it leaves you plenty of room to move. Wear the stuff you think you'll have on underneath, and maybe a little more, and make sure you can still spud a hole, crank an auger, and bend to fight a fish.

BENEATH THE SUIT

In the past no discussion of ice-fishing clothing was complete without a lecture on layering—wearing multiple, carefully chosen pieces of clothing that could be added or removed to match changing weather conditions and activity levels. That's still good advice, and it's easier than ever to follow, with ice-fishing suit makers offering their own brands of super under- and mid-layer garments.

For all but the coldest of weather, thanks to the advances in outerwear described above, most styles and materials of long johns work well beneath it. Polypropylene and woolen blends lead the way today.

Many anglers won't give up their blue jeans, wearing them under their ice-fishing outerwear. But experts say denim has little insulating value, gets wet easily, stays clammy long, and doesn't add much warmth.

Instead, pull on a pair of corduroy trousers or, better yet, a pair of woolen ones, if you need a middle layer. Honestly? I seldom wear more than a pair of wool-blend long johns beneath my ice bibs.

Up top, I like a long-john top and an Irish fisherman's wool sweater beneath my ice parka, and I can fish in temperatures well below zero in relative comfort.

Hands and Feet

I once insisted on mittens for ice fishing, their whole-hand approach maintaining more warmth. That was before today's ice-fishing gloves came on the scene to provide both splendid warmth and flexibility.

Pick mittens or gloves that easily cover the cuffs of your coat. A narrow slice of exposed wrist skin seems to chill your entire body, as well as your enthusiasm for fishing. Make sure you can remove the mitts or gloves easily when fishing action really gets going. Beyond that, find a pair that feels good; you may have them awhile. I still have leather fleece-lined mitts that I purchased an astonishing forty-five years ago! I treat them each season or two with a good waterproofing paste and have never had them soak through.

Obviously, a good pair of mitts is a sound ice-fishing investment. Don't think this a knock on gloves, by the way, if they're the right gloves. I've become a fan of a pair of heavy Fish Monkey–brand gloves that have kept my hands cozy at 20 below zero.

Military surplus stores provided many of us with Korean War–era boots, extremely heavy but waterproof and supremely warm. They were called Mickey Mouse boots for their bulbous shapes, and the white ones were reputedly more cold-resistant than the black. Both were prodigiously heavy when plodding across a lake, but a pair of Mickey Mouse boots over a couple pairs of heavy socks practically guaranteed warm feet.

Mickey Mouse boots edged out the four-buckle arctic overshoes and felt liners my dad and grandfathers wore. Both took a back seat to the felt-pac snowmobile boots that came on the market, affordably, in that sport's first boom in the 1970s. From them emerged waterproof boots made especially for ice fishing.

And now, there are splendid, thick-soled boots designed specifically for long days of ice fishing. Most ice-fishing boots today have removable felt liners, making it simple to dry out any perspiration before the next day's fishing. Others are insulated with Thinsulate or other synthetic insulation. Many are waterproof, and some top-shelf ice-fishing boots are even made of waterproof, breathable material, for maximum comfort. Set your priorities—lightweightedness, waterproofness, traction, cost—and there's a high-quality boot design that dials it in.

Remember when shopping that the most important place for insulation is between the bottom of your feet and the top of the ice; air has far less effect on your foot temperature than the surface on which your feet rest. Here's a tip: Before giving up on the boots you already own, try adding an insulated insole. That extra buffer between your feet and the ice may be all you need.

As in all things ice fishing, the modern marketplace offers a range of comfortable, secure creepers or cleats to provide added traction moving across the ice. A slip on the ice can become a serious fall, and cleats need not be mountaineering quality to reduce drastically the possibility of that slip. Buy *and wear* cleats: The only time I ever suffered a cleat-related injury was when I fell while walking my dog and landed my hip bone on the city sidewalk—on the cleats I was carrying in my pocket, not wearing on my feet.

Socks are another challenge. You'll need to find the combination of socks that works best for you. In years past I favored wool socks, a couple of pairs of them. I'd carry them along on the drive to the lake and put them on when we parked; that would avoid a build-up of perspiration along the way. Recently, a couple of companies have brought to market socks and other clothing made with the underhairs of American bison, a material they refer to as "bison down." Bison down socks from both the Buffalo Wool Co. and United by Blue have become my go-to cold-weather footgear. Merino and Smartwool are solid ice-fishing choices as liners and main socks, too.

CHAPTER 5

Two-Flop Days

THERE ARE ALL TYPES OF ICE-FISHING DAYS. GREAT DAYS AND BAD DAYS. Fun days and tough days. Fishy days and skunky days. Balmy days and two-flop days.

Through most of the winter, the ice angler doesn't actually suffer very much. Folks at home may shudder at the thought of their loved ones at the mercy of the elements on a big, windswept lake. But the truth is that, with modern cold-weather clothing and boots, most winter days provide pretty comfortable fishing.

Comfortable, anyway, compared to two-flop days.

My first two-flop day was experienced on a lake from which we'd been extracting crappies with stunning regularity. Day after day, 9-inch and larger crappies seemed to line up for a shot at the teardrop lure baited with a wax worm, and the tasty panfish quickly piled up, flopping against each other on the ice.

This day was different, though. We first noticed it when we walked onto the frozen lake and, instead of feeling our hands and feet warm with the exertion of a quarter-mile hike through the snow, we stopped to pull our hats lower over our ears and zip up our coats.

The wind slapped our faces angrily. Undaunted, finally we settled over the productive fishing holes we'd punched a few days earlier. The spud made short work of the 3 inches of ice that had formed since sundown the preceding day. And pulling the 4-pound test monofilament between gloves seemed to take the cold-induced kinks out of it. The wax worms

On bitter-cold, "two-flop" days, ice forms quickly in the hole and on the line.

were stiff, but rolling them between the fingers—in the few seconds we allowed those digits to be exposed—restored the baits to softness so they could be threaded onto a hook. Now, we fished.

I didn't really pay too much attention to the first few crappies we iced. They were coming atop the ice at the same rate we'd enjoyed in previous days. But after we'd caught a half dozen, I noticed there was no movement on the pile.

A 10-incher struck my lure, was elevated to ice-top, and joined the mound. It flopped once at full-strength, again half-heartedly, and then appeared to freeze solid.

"Who needs a thermometer?" my friend asked, rhetorically. "We know it's a two-flop day!"

Temperature readings mean little to the ice angler. I've been cozy at 10°F, when the sun shone brightly and the winds lay still. And I've shivered when winds sped 35° air across the lake.

Celsius? Fahrenheit? Nah. Not anymore. We've fixed upon the "Flop" scale, the number of times a fresh-caught panfish flops on the ice.

We quit counting after three flops. That's a blue-ribbon ice-fishing day. Slush won't form in the minnow bucket. Checking tip-up holes every fifteen or twenty minutes will ensure they'll stay open enough that you can easily extract the machine if a fish hits. Ice will be slow to form on your jigging-rod bobber, too, so that you won't often have to suck on the float to remove enough ice to allow you to fish efficiently. Same with the tip guide of your spinning rod, which in harsh weather clogs with ice.

The three-flop day or better lets you know how good you've got it. A gentle tap will puncture the skim ice sealing your minnows in the bucket. After an hour's fishing you might slip on your gloves for a little warming before returning to barehanded fishing. You might even leave the hood of your parka down, tucking it along the back of your neck.

That hood comes up on a two-flop day, even if you don't have to pull the drawstrings tight. You'll wear gloves more than half the time, and make sure your back is against the wind. If there's a shanty nearby, you may decide that the best fishing spot is just downwind of it.

Woe to the angler who heads out unprepared mentally and physically on a one-flop day, though, when the bluegill, crappie, walleye, or trout freezes after just one wiggle on the ice, and you can stand to remove your gloves only briefly. On this day the wind seems positively mean-spirited, lashing your face on the walk onto the ice and almost invariably coming around 180 degrees to dish out the same punishment on the way back in. Thin monofilament or fluorocarbon line seems to spin into knots easier on this kind of day, and you'll wish you brought extra fishing rigs so you could untangle snarled ones later at your warm home instead of trying to fix them here. On a one-flop day, your feet quit stinging after an hour's fishing, and only later will you realize they're not comfortable but numb.

In fact, you know you're getting warmer on a one-flop day when your feet and hands start hurting again.

There are even no-flop days.

We were heading 80 miles to a trout lake one morning when we heard on the radio that a neighboring school district's classes had been canceled because of severe cold. A regular fishing buddy taught in that district, so in those pre-cell-phone days we decided to stop at his house and invite him along, even though it was only 6 a.m. Our faith proved well placed: Aware that we'd planned to fish, he was watching for us out the living room window when we pulled into his driveway.

It was cold on the lake, fishing in the open, sitting on upturned pails. Bitterly, painfully cold. Minnows froze in the bucket, and tip-ups were locked in ice in fifteen minutes. The fishing was OK. We fought fish with gloved hands, shucked ice from the tip-up, and somehow the trout didn't simply break the 4-pound test line. When the trout we caught hit the ice, they never flopped, quivered, or anything. They quick-froze, pure and simple.

We tended tip-ups for several hours. One bearded fisherman had his breath freeze on and between his mustache and beard until the two were fused together. Another gave up after having been forced to spud two tip-ups free of the rapidly forming ice just to check them.

When those two finally surrendered to the harsh elements, they found your author in the small car, trying to thaw a frozen camera on the defroster.

Driving off to a warm restaurant, we turned on the car radio and learned that now, at high noon, the actual temperature had risen—to 20 below zero with a windchill reading of 50 below!

Then we heard a strange noise from the back seat.

One of the trout had thrashed in a pail.

"You hear that?" Tom asked with a laugh. "It's not a no-flop day after all!"

CHAPTER 6

Electronics

ON MANY ICE-FISHING PARKAS, THERE STILL HANGS A CLIP-ON WEIGHT, originally brightly painted, that an angler would attach to a lure or hook and lower to the bottom of a lake.

That measured the depth. One might then adjust a float or otherwise fix the length, or measure the distance in peg windings, reel cranks, or arm pulls.

You tried to remember that measurement, because additional tests would determine how it changed as one moved across the lake. You'd map a rudimentary mental chart; lake maps available then were only marginally more complete.

Fish-cover insights? There might be weeds on the clip-on "depth finder" when it was retrieved. But more likely one would collect clues while fishing—bits of weed on a hook or a lure lost to brush.

Then there was the question of fish, generically and specifically, whether they were present and if so, what they were, answered only by looking into the water from within a lightproof shanty or shelter, or by lying on the ice, coat over one's head, and hoping the water was shallow enough and clear enough to see what might be swimming below.

How stark the contrast with how we gather ice-fishing information today! You can assemble as much electronic assistance as your tastes, lugging ability, and budget allow, at each stage removing question marks and fleshing out your fishing strategy.

Watching a flasher for information on fish and the lure, an angler can quickly remove the transducer to make way for icing a fish.

I recall laughing after peering into the screen of an Aqua-Vu portable camera on a dogsled-transported fishing trip into the Boundary Waters Canoe Wilderness Area in northern Minnesota.

Tim Lesmeister, a longtime friend and the trip's organizer, had connections at the company that made the then-new underwater camera system (and continues to lead the way to new innovations). He'd brought along this camera, its screen mounted in a largish plastic box and its lens dangling on a long cable. Several of us quickly forgot about the below-zero cold, the long distance from civilization, the dogs sleeping on straw nearby, even the wolves we'd heard howling the night before, as we took turns staring past the sun shield and into the hollow that housed the screen, watching our lures and baits and, in time, how trout and pike reacted to them.

My laugh? Without fail, as we took our turns, we each became so fixated on the scene that we forgot to set the hook when a fish struck!

Any kid with a mask and snorkel can tell you: There's mystery in what goes on underwater and magic in seeing it. The modern ice angler enjoys that same sense of wonder, whether watching a camera image or "seeing" through information displayed on a sonar device.

My wife doesn't like to see the fish she's trying to catch, or even the lack of fish in waters she's fishing. She fishes on faith, eschewing fish-finders, cameras, and even polarized glasses except for eye protection, and I can't knock that. She knows what she likes—the mystery more than its early unmasking.

I, though, want to know what's down there and to get every possible leg up on catching it! And it's become steadily easier each ice-fishing year to put my eyes on the prize.

THE SONAR SOLUTION

Just as radar emits and times the return of a radio-wave signal in air to sketch an image of what it's struck and where, sonar times a sound's return to show and tell what's underwater.

There are two main types of sonar units in ice-fishing use: fish sounders (or "flashers") and fish-finders. Both make splendid ice-fishing tools, with slightly different selling points. Either, equipped with a transducer suspended from a float so it shoots directly down the hole, can make your ice fishing more efficient and enjoyable.

A fish sounder provides instant information on water depth and fish in the narrow column directly beneath you, displayed as illuminated lines on a circular display. You can infer the bottom type by the light patterns, colors, and intensities (the brighter and more compact the light, the harder the bottom, for example) and can watch even a small lure and a fish's reaction to it.

When flashers first hit the ice in a big way, ice-fishing pioneer Dave Genz even developed special lures for Lindy–Little Joe, including the Genz Worm, Fat Boy, Pounder, and Coped, bulky and heavy enough to show up on electronic sounders. "With skinny lures like the traditional teardrop," said Genz of the standard class of panfish lures, "you had to turn up the gain (how strongly the fish-finder amplified the signal it received) to see it, and you got all kinds of interference, zooplankton and stuff." He described his new lures as "flasher-friendly lures," and many of today's most popular lures are similarly designed with sonar in mind.

Thanks to the evolution in electronic equipment and the lures themselves, it's easy to monitor what's going on down there!

Watch a tiny jig and wax worm as you wiggle it 18 feet down. Unmolested, it appears as a band in one color on the flasher dial. Then a fish arrives, probably displayed in another color. Jig the lure and the fish may draw closer yet to the bait, the combined readings a more intense color yet. Or it may dash away—and you know there's something it disliked. Monitoring all those, you can track the fish's reaction to repeat the winning presentation, and avoid duplicating the losing one, all day long.

Even better detail is available in the near-bottom zone in which many fish lurk. Most sounders and finders have zoom options, focusing on a specific range of depths. Some automatically adjust their electronic gaze to the bottom 6 feet of water, and many offer split-screen options: the zoom segment on one side, the complete water column on the other.

The level of detail provided by today's ice-fishing electronics is marvelous. Where we were once pleased that we could see a medium-size lure on a display, with today's technology I can sometimes tell when a wax worm has been stolen from a teardrop!

A fish-finder is just as detailed and nearly as swift as a flasher, and it can provide historical info, GPS (Global Positioning System) navigation, mapping, and other features the flasher can't. The fish-finder collects data from a generally wider cone than a flasher and processes it through a small computer. You can select display features, from a graph-like display that shows changes over time to a convincing simulation of a flasher dial. You can display lake and regional maps and your location upon them, and with some units even collect, store, and manipulate your own map-making data.

Some top manufacturers offer both flashers and fish-finders. Their finders, with flexible displays and CHIRP (Concentrated High Intensity Radar Pulse), produce results similar to those of flashers, plus add GPS, mapping, and other informational options.

CHIRP? Until recently, ice sonar units operated at specific frequency rates, some with dual-frequency transducers. You could toggle between low frequency, with its wider beam and deeper depth reading, and high frequency, with a narrow beam and enhanced ability to pick up details. Then along came CHIRP, sending a series of pulses that each contain a range of frequencies, for outstanding data fish-finder display.

My everyday unit, a Humminbird Ice Helix 5, has dual CHIRP spectrum capability, three-quarter-inch target separation, and the ability to create Auto Chart—a way to make my own maps of favorite fishing spots. I think it presents fishing information just as reliably as my buddy's splendid Vexilar F28 flasher—and can provide me the mapping and navigating info his can't. He's just as loyal to his Vexilar.

Next level? Humminbird Mega Live and Mega 360, Garmin Live-Scope and Panoptix, and similar systems from other manufacturers that provide real-time, detailed, and extensive views of what's happening beneath an angler, or in any desired direction. They comprise software and hardware including accessory transducers compatible with specific fish-finders. Originally designed to mount on boat hulls or electric trolling motors, they can now be lowered beneath an ice hole on special mounts. It's expensive technology—$1,000 and quickly much higher—and calls for considerable battery power, but it's a real eye-opener and a crowd-pleaser. Guides, especially, have embraced it.

When guide Alex Peterson brought his into the permanent shanty in which we fished on Minnesota's Lake of the Woods, we could watch fish approach and take our lures and baits, as if it were televised! We could even identify fish by species.

So, what's it gonna be: flasher or finder?

Just as boaters continue to argue the merits of two-stroke vs. four-stroke power while the differences in size, weight, performance, and price have all shrunk, ice anglers have maintained system and brand loyalties while the differences between fish sounders and fish-finders—at least for "marking" fish, lake bottoms, and lures—become more arcane each season.

The main difference, to me, is that the finder can do the work of a flasher and more, with screens that can show sonar history, perform GPS navigation, and even craft personalized lake maps. My Humminbird, matched to an ice-fishing transducer, is otherwise the same basic model as is on my trolling boat, so I only have to learn and remember one set of commands. The two units also share an accessory map chip, and each stands as ready backup if the other fails.

But yes, sounders such as the legendary Vexilar still beat finders to the punch, presenting information in real time instead of delaying it a bit for processing into a sounder-style format. But the difference is slighter than ever. Vexilar fans are fiercely loyal: My buddy Cliff swears, "If I got to the lake and found I'd forgotten my Vexilar, I'd go home." Even, I suspect, if he were offered the option of borrowing my fish-finder or a spare.

Another friend, fishing educator Mark Martin, fishes exclusively with Marcum fish-finders and cameras. Garmin fans are just as committed.

As in outboard motors and reels, it's harder each year to find a bad one on the market.

Some say a fish-finder is less rugged than a sounder. In my experience they both handle far more abuse than we should give them!

Lights! Camera! Action!

Lower an underwater camera on its tethering cable, watch the screen topside, and you've got a window on that under-ice world. You know just what the bottom looks like, what swims above it, and how that creature reacts to your lure and the action you impart to it.

Fishing cameras come in two main styles: large-screen units that run off standard 12-volt ice-fishing batteries, and pocket-sized cameras that carry small rechargeable batteries on board. The former are much easier to view but large, similar in size to a fish-finder. The smaller units are handy, although they're a bit more difficult to see in the sun and have almost a claustrophobic feel to their images.

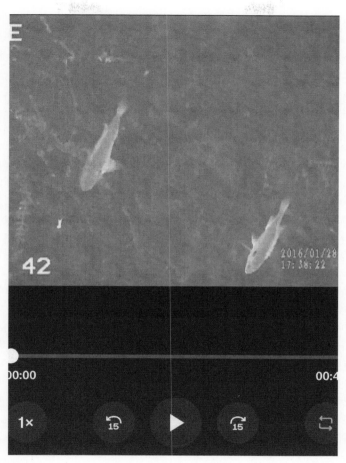

An underwater camera can provide insight on bottom structure, the presence of fish, and how they react to a bait (left).

I've owned one of each in recent years and still own (and use sometimes, but not all the time) a pocket-sized Aqua-Vu Micro Revolution. A larger unit traveled to Maine, where a friend adds it to gear lugged behind his snowmobile and loves to watch trout and burbot on it.

I agreed with Mark Martin when we chatted off-season about cameras: "They help people understand fish reactions," Mark said. "What a lure looks like underwater, exactly what the structure is, things like that. If someone used one for a year, and you took it away from them, they'd know what to do if they didn't have it, just from what they've learned." And they might well return to it to learn more from time to time! Forced to choose between sonar and video, though, I think most ice anglers would grab their flasher or finder.

There may be anglers who enjoy watching a camera screen all day, but I'm not one of them. Remember that sled-dog-ice-fishing story at the start of this chapter, when one after another we were so transfixed by the then-new camera that we forgot to catch the fish? The risk remains real.

I like burning a mental image into my brain—the structure, the fish, the lure and its action—and then using that as background as I watch my line, rod tip, and fish-finder readout.

But a fresh visit with a camera each season, or when visiting a new spot, helps the angler locate features like weed-bed edges and pockets within weed beds, which can be super fishing zones. Watching a lure's response to your jigging motions, and a fish's reaction to both, can be a real eye-opener. Knowing the species of the fish beneath you can be a great aid.

"The camera has taught me some things," modern ice-fishing pioneer Dave Genz told me long ago. "It's not magic, but it has taught me things."

It taught him that fish often show up as soon as a hole is drilled, for example, rather than being frightened away from the action. That encourages him to keep moving through the day, unafraid of chasing fish away at each stop.

Watching fish react to specific jigging actions has taught him to jig a lure aggressively at midday, when fish are often reluctant to bite. "Three snaps and hold. Three snaps and hold. In the daytime, if you give a fish the opportunity to examine a lure, that's exactly what it does. I snap it to make him bite."

And sometimes, smile for the camera!

CHAPTER 7

Panfish

THE TINY BOBBER DID LITTLE MORE THAN QUIVER. MY PARTNER'S EYES caught the slight movement, though, and his body tensed, his attention riveted to the 6-inch-wide hole in the 5-inch-thick ice. He raised the jigging rod just high enough to remove the slack between its tip and the little float. And when the line quivered and the bobber wriggled ever so slightly, again he struck, folding the light rod into an arc, then dropping it to the ice as he grabbed the light line.

The fight itself was quick. After all, only about 6 feet of line separated Dale from his adversary. Still, my buddy tugged on the fish gingerly, especially as it came closer to the surface. Then he slipped his hand into the water, just far enough to flip onto the ice a 7-inch bluegill.

The fish, brightly arrayed in blues, greens, and yellows, flopped once or twice on the ice before coming to rest against a dozen or so of its colleagues. Dale smiled admiringly, rebaited his hook, and lowered the lure again toward the bottom.

Fun time today, fish fry tomorrow! But in many ways this was yesteryear.

The ballet played out between ice angler and panfish retains its grace, but the staging has changed substantially since the scene described above. You can still catch plenty of bluegills, sunfish, and other panfish on a simple, inexpensive fishing rod with light line wrapped on pegs and threaded through a bobber, but even the entry-level bluegiller today often opts for a nice fishing rod and a dependable reel. The bite is most likely transmitted through the line and the sensitive, solid fiberglass or graphite

Many an ice angler's goal: a hand-sized bluegill

rod, or with the help of a strike indicator of delicate, springy metal or wire. The line might be monofilament nylon, such as my buddy used, or near-invisible fluorocarbon, or even wispy-thin braided line. His lure was a simple, painted, teardrop-shaped lead jig, either vertical or horizontal in presentation, and baited with a natural grub. But today's angler has seemingly a million choices of lure styles, shapes, colors, and materials—and a rack of top-quality plastic live-bait imitations, most of them more wigglingly enticing in the water than the creature they imitate.

So yes, the basics of light line, gentle jigging, close attention, and cautious battle still apply as they did when my friend gathered his catch of panfish. But today's angler, even on their first day out, enjoys great advantages.

Many of us launched our fishing careers by triumphantly capturing a panfish—bluegill, sunfish, white or black crappie, rock bass, white bass, or yellow perch. The fish, all but the perch a saucer-shaped fish, was a trophy, no matter how long or how short, and its capture darned-near guaranteed that we'd be back for more. Sure, most first catches probably came from the open waters of a warmwater, warm-weather lake, but ice panfishing gets into your blood just as easily.

Like its summer counterpart, the winter panfish is a willing feeder; seldom will an angler get completely skunked. It's a scrappy battler, too; on light tackle you'll never be sure of defeating a panfish until it's on the ice, and even then I've seen more than one flop its way across the ice, back into the hole and away to freedom. And the panfish is sure a welcome, tasty contribution to the dinner table; I wouldn't trade the first mess of winter-caught panfish for any other fish dinner, any time of the year. And even though fish are theoretically less active in winter than summer, I've seen more periods of nonstop fishing action through the ice than I've witnessed in open water.

FIRST, THE WHYS

Your favorite bluegill or crappie lake is ice-covered and has been that way for several weeks. A blanket of snow probably covers it, too. Both factors come quickly to bear on the fish beneath that ice. Lakes get oxygen from two sources: contact with the air and the production of oxygen by green plants growing underwater. Remember photosynthesis from that high school biology class? Come winter, shorter days and ice and snow cover reduce the amount of sunlight reaching green plants, and they turn dead or dormant. Their decay consumes oxygen, where their growth once produced it, and when oxygen becomes scarce, fish become less active.

Another change takes place within your favorite lake in winter, too. The water, naturally, has cooled. Fish are cold-blooded and, like all creatures of that type, match their metabolism or body activity to their environment. When the water turns cool, that too makes the fish less active.

A summer bluegill will submerge a clunky 2-inch-diameter bobber and keep right on going. But some of the winter's most productive action comes only after the angler has learned to watch for the tiny sign of a strike. Winter panfish don't hit hard, don't stick around long, and take a bait quite gently. If you snooze, you lose. Light tackle gives you the best odds of fooling that fish, sensing its strike, and enjoying a scrappy, light-action battle.

You don't need heavy gear anyway. I've caught northern pike 2 feet long through the ice on my light panfish gear. Every year some big bass are brought atop the ice on light tackle. Ditto for walleyes. We iced a 7-pound carp one winter day when it decided a wax worm threaded onto a teardrop hook looked good. Winter fish, especially those of the warm-water variety, aren't nearly as apt to bust up your tackle as summer fish. It's all because of that winter slowdown of metabolism.

The bluegill that inhaled a popping bug with such gusto last summer is semi-dormant, not moving around as much, and not all that hungry. It might pause and snatch a small morsel during its limited tours but not likely a big meal. And it's usually not rushing to that dinner either, except on those rare and delightful occasions when winter panfish seem to go on a feeding binge.

But just as the lake's oxygen factory has shut down for the winter, the food factory is nearly idle, too. Particularly in early winter and late winter, there's more hunger than food. That makes your bait more attractive and your winter angling days so productively enjoyable. You're likely also paying more attention to your fishing than you do in the summer. After all, there's no ball game on the radio, you can't stretch out and catch a suntan, and it's too cold to drink beer. About the only reason to be on a winter lake is to fish. So you concentrate and do a better job.

Generally, if you want to catch panfish through the ice, you're going to have to match your tackle and tactics to the fish and its lifestyle: smaller baits, less movement, and more delicacy. You're going to have to work harder and be both more patient and more attentive.

In fact, I'd bet your summer success, good as it may be, would improve if you used lighter tackle and approached that warm-weather fishing as if it were ice fishing!

Panfish Tackle: Sticks, Rods, and Reels

Initially, let's lump all the panfish together—bluegills, sunfish, white and black crappies, even rock and white bass. Often, several species will swim in the same lake, and the same basic tackle and tactics will take all of them.

As your parents, grandparents, and great-grandparents may have, you can still catch plenty of panfish and have plenty of fun with a simple rod with line-winding pegs or bracket, no reel. Plenty of ice anglers still do. Early in my ice-fishing career, we had two choices for panfish gear: build a wooden- or cork-handled rod for ourselves from broken or obsolete rod tips, or, for a few dollars, buy a fiberglass rod, likely with a wooden handle and one guide besides the tip top, probably from a bait shop. Line storage was the job of wooden pegs, a snap-on bracket, or a simple plastic reel. Wooden sticks with L-shaped nails for line-winding were another, even clumsier, option.

When talking about the good old days, these weren't them.

Gradually, rod manufacturers learned that ice anglers would spend good money for good gear, while those fishers were learning they had better luck and more fun using good tackle. Solid fiberglass and graphite rods, less likely to break under harsh conditions than hollow, open-water rods, came onto the market, matched to increasingly reliable spinning reels. Then came the in-line reel, a cross between a fly reel and a center pin reel, that would take up and release line without imparting a twist to it. Anglers who watched panfish reactions from darkhouses or on camera had noticed that a spinning lure often spooked fish. Here was a solution! (Many anglers use in-line reels in water of 20 feet or less, spinning gear for deeper efforts, where its quicker retrieval and efficiency outweighs any spin.)

Today's panfish specialist hits the ice with rods and reels of equal quality to those of the open-water angler, rods with price tags that quickly reach $50 and soar well beyond, and reels to match. They fill pails and rod cases with rods from 2-footers for easy handling within a portable shelter, to 5 feet or more for sneaking a lure into a hole over shallow water.

"It is amazing how many ice fishermen are still fishing with their grandfather's equipment and are proud of it," ice-fishing pioneer Dave Genz told me while showing off some new ice rods he'd helped design for a major tackle company. "It's good to be proud of the old equipment," he said while we filled a pail with foot-long perch, "but not so good to fish with it." Modern ice rods, he boasted, have all the features of a fine open-water rod in an ice-fishing format.

What's My Line?

Of all the panfisher's tackle, line may be easiest to overlook. Keep it light. Winter panfishing requires a more subtle approach than its summer counterpart.

I don't use monofilament nylon or fluorocarbon line heavier than 4 pounds test for panfish. Three-pound is better, and two-pound test is best of all, once you've learned to handle the light stuff. Start with 3-pound: It will work on all but the most skittish fish and is relatively easy to handle. You can lighten up later if fishing conditions demand it.

New lines have been created specific to ice fishing, in monofilament, fluorocarbon, cofilament (the former in a sheath of the latter), and braided materials. Fluoro's nearly invisible, both to the fish (good) and to the knot-tying angler (challenging), and braid is virtually non-stretch for detecting the slightest bite but ices up frustratingly when used outdoors. Overall, it seems to me that more ice anglers are spooling up with ice-formulated fluorocarbon line each season.

But, as in many things ice fishing, you and I may well see things differently: Try a few lines and see which works best for you. But a soft mono or fluoro, in 2, 3, or 4 pounds test, will never let you down.

Braided line in ice-fishing weights has become popular, but it requires the Palomar or other special knot instead of the double-improved clinch many mono- or fluoro-fishing anglers prefer. Whatever line material you select, the box or the manufacturer's website is sure to offer step-by-step guides to knots that work well with it.

Goodbye, Bobber? Not Yet!

One sees fewer bobbers on the ice than in the days before fine-tuned rods, reels, and lines (which together allow one to more easily feel or see bites), but they're still a good way to launch an ice-fishing career. A bobber teaches.

Begin with a peg-type ice-fishing bobber, round or nearly so, with a hole drilled through the center through which the fishing line runs.

An angler uses an in-line reel and a spring strike indicator in a hunt for panfish.

A wooden or plastic peg presses into the hole to secure the line. You want the smallest float that will hold your lure and bait afloat; the proper matchup may shift as you change lure and bait styles through the day.

I couldn't count the times that my small peg-type bobber would, instead of standing straight, tip slightly to one side or lie flat on its side. I'd set the hook and, more times than not, feel the resistance of a fighting panfish at the other end. The fish had approached the bait from alongside or below, gently inhaled it, and remained beneath the bobber, lifting it slightly. That let the float tip over, and I set the hook. No summer-style push-button bobber would ever have told me about the strikes. The best bobber for ice fishing for panfish is the smallest peg-type float that will hold your bait off bottom. Dime-sized is about the maximum.

Spring-type strike indicators, in effect continuations of the rod that flex to show the slightest bite, never go out of style. Schooley brand bobbers were flat steel, and those several decades old still do the trick. Piano-wire designs, though, such as the spring indicators offered by St. Croix and featured on some of their splendid ice rods, are supremely sensitive and would be my choice if limited to one type of bite indicator. But I have several super-light panfish rods, too, that are so supple they do the job themselves. And I get out an old bobber stick now and then, too, just for grins!

THE LURE(S) OF PANFISHING

The panfish standard was once the teardrop-shaped, molded-lead lure, baited with a grub (wax worm, spike, corn borer, mousie, or wiggler), or even with a minnow. Teardrops come in a vast variety of solid colors and patterns, and if limited to a few, I'd pack some in red, bright orange, chartreuse, and white, trying different colors until I found what produced the best on that particular day.

But like everything else ice fishing, the panfish lure offerings of your local tackle shop, big-box sporting goods store, or online tackle dealer have exploded. With new shapes—from bug-eyed jigs in flattened or squatty shapes that make them more visible to sonar, to blade-shaped lures with minnow-image sides, or entire lines of lures made of tungsten to sink quickly, even through slush, while dodging lead concerns—your choice of panfish ice lures rivals that of the summer trout fly fisher. Every day and lake has its top lure, likely reflecting nuances in the food supply, and nearly every lure has its day, too. Start with a small selection recommended by local experts, and experiment each time out. It's a great chunk of the fun!

WEIGHT LOSS

I'll only use split shot when absolutely necessary. There may be times when it's just too windy to feed line into a hole without extra weight. Sometimes active minnows require some weight to keep them in place.

But unless absolutely essential, leave the shot off the line, as it tends to muffle both your feel for the action and visual indicators of same.

A SPARE OR A PAIR

That's really about all there is to rigging up. To catch panfish through the ice, you need only one jigging rod, so-equipped. But again, it's a good idea to keep changing lures throughout the day, until you find the size, shape, and color panfish favor most. You can, of course, snip off the unproductive lure and tie on another, but I'd rather keep my fingers warm for rebaiting hooks and unhooking fish. I'll often walk onto the ice with a half dozen jigging rods jammed into a five-gallon plastic pail. Our state law allows an angler to fish with up to three lines, but there's nothing wrong with having others at the ready. If one lure doesn't produce, I switch rods instead of changing lures. The selection of rods is further insurance against a calamity befalling any one rod, line, or lure.

LOCATING PANFISH

Finally, now you're ready for the ice, warmly clothed, sure of the safety of the ice, armed with a spud or auger and one or more jigging rods. Where on your chosen lake will you begin fishing?

Panfish and panfish anglers are similarly gregarious. Crappies and sunfish, including bluegills, gather in species or combined schools to pursue their food-hunting and other activities. Panfish anglers form clusters atop the ice over productive fishing spots and, provided you're courteous, probably won't mind you joining them.

That makes the first part of your fishing trip a little easier. If your lake, like most, boasts a few tight clusters of anglers, start near one of them. Chances are good the anglers are assembled there because the fish are, too.

When I approach a group of anglers, I mentally compute the distance they've allowed between each other, and then make sure I don't bore a hole closer than that distance from any one of them. Provided you drill your holes as quickly and quietly as possible, keep your kids or dog from harassing others, and don't play a loud radio, your angling neighbors are likely to flash you a smile instead of a glare.

On your own, look for panfish to cluster wherever the bottom changes or some structure offers them protection. Drop-offs, especially those that fall from chest- or head-high water into depths of 10 to 20 feet, are always good bets. So are sunken brush piles, areas in impounded lakes where logs lie on bottom, weed-bed edges, holes within weed beds, or, especially in midwinter, deeper holes in the lake.

On my own favorite panfish lake—now lost to a dam failure—we'd begin the season at a familiar spot less than 15 yards from shore, where the bottom sharply dropped to about 12 feet of water. Crappies and blue-gills would mix about evenly in the catch. After a couple of weeks, the action and our attention gradually moved several hundred yards offshore, each stop in a little deeper water. Bluegill action tapered off as we fished 25-foot depths, but the crappies more than made up for it. From this spot road-builders had scooped up gravel before the dam was built, and crappies loved hanging over the basin in midwinter.

Much about this pattern will ring familiar to many ice anglers, but you really wouldn't have to know all that background to find this spot and catch fish from it; there were always a dozen or more fish shanties clustered tightly over the basin spot, with several dozen anglers toiling outside them.

But suppose I didn't see any groups of anglers on a lake I was to fish, didn't know the lake, and didn't have a map showing its contour? I'd start near shore, in waters 3 to 8 feet deep, and give panfish ten or fifteen minutes to go for one of my top-producing teardrops or small jigs, baited with a natural or plastic grub and fished from the bottom to about halfway to the surface. I'd switch to a different offering for ten or fifteen minutes, and try to talk a partner into trying the same or a similar spot with different-shaded lures. If those efforts produced no action, I'd move, and I'd keep moving and switching baits until I located fish, or tested all waters up to about 30 feet deep. Obviously, input from a sonar unit or underwater camera would help shorten this process. If all that didn't work, I'd try a different portion of the lake, a different lake, or a different activity. There are times when all the fish in a specific lake seem to go off their feed at the same time. Most days, though, you can find at least a few willing fish.

On most outings the bulk of your panfish catch, especially bluegills and other sunfish, will come from near the bottom, usually within a foot of it. So make sure you're fishing in that zone.

If you don't have an electronic flasher or fish-finder, check the depth by clipping your depth-finding weight to your unbaited lure and release line until the weight touches bottom. You can mark the spot with a slip bobber stop and reel in, or just measure the distance with arm-pulls of line. If fishing with a peg bobber (and no reel), remove the bobber's peg before letting out the line and weight until slack line tells you you're on bottom. Now slowly retrieve line until it's just snug, and replace the peg. Pull line through the bobber equal to the distance from bottom you want to fish, and remove the clip-on weight. Your bobber will hold your lure and bait exactly that far off bottom each time you remove a fish and return the offering to the productive zone.

BAITING UP FOR PANFISH

Grub baits are my first choice for panfish. Fish don't steal them as easily as they do minnows, and you don't need to get your hands wet to rebait. Oh, and panfish love them!

Wax worms and spikes are available in almost all ice-country bait shops, spikes even in a variety of colors. Other grub options include mousies, acorn and corn borers, and goldenrod grubs. Wigglers have their fans, especially for perch.

Many wax-worm fans are adamant about the way they bait up, sliding the grub onto the hook without pushing it past the point. If the tip of the point shows, they insist, you'll cut your action at least by half. It sounds crazy, and I can't guess why a shiny lure attracts fish but a shiny hook point puts them off. But I was taught to cover the point, and whether it's truth or just tradition, I don't feel right fishing waxies any other way.

Spike fans, meanwhile, press the point through the flat end of the grub and let the bait dangle. Some even keep adding spikes until they've created what they call a "chandelier." With six or seven maggots dangling off the hook, they catch tons of fish, too. One friend uses several different colors in a chandelier, though insisting that at least one of them be red.

As we'll say often about ice fishing: You'll fish best with what you believe in.

If fishing with minnows—far more productive for crappies than for sunfish—you can hook the minnow just under the dorsal fin or, especially with small minnows, through the head. Small minnows die quickly, so the jigging action you give the lure is often as important as the natural action of the baitfish.

Not that everything has to be natural. A new generation of plastic ice-fishing baits—grubs, minnows, and other critters—have come on strong, often outfishing the natural creatures they simulate.

Many anglers thread the entire body of a fake bait onto a hook, much like they would with a jig-and-grub combination in summer. But barely securing the tip of the bait to the hook leaves it free to flex, and the resulting lively action achieved by just the ever-present current in the water can turn lookers into biters.

Maki and other manufacturers have created formulations specifically for cold-water fishing, rendering plastics as soft as live baits.

With either plastic baits or dyed natural grubs, experiment to find the day's hot color—the one fish inhale instead of just mouthing. That turns bites into catches.

Jigging Tips

Lower the bait, carefully watching the line as you do. Sometimes we've found fish suspended off bottom just by noting slack forming in the line as it's being lowered. Any time the line acts funny, set the hook, just to be sure. And if you hook a suspended fish, note the depth so you can return to it for more action.

When the lure and bait have reached bottom or other desired depth, begin a gentle jigging motion, keeping the lure moving much of the time. I usually lift the rod tip a couple of inches, several times in a row, then let the bait and lure settle back into place. Occasionally I raise the bait a couple of feet, letting the lure flutter back down. And I'm always watching. If the line or strike indicator acts the least bit unusual, especially if the float lies on its side or the rod tip or strike indicator shows less tension, it's probably because a fish has nailed the bait on the way down.

Remember: If you think you might be having a bite while panfishing, you probably are.

HARDWARE FOR CRAPPIES

Crappies are more reliant on minnows and other small fish than sunfish are, and the ice angler who expands the tackle box to include smaller spoons—especially those with glow finishes, light sticks, or built-in rattles—often reaps fishy benefits. Smaller versions of such minnow-imitating lures as Jigging Rapalas and Northland's Puppet Minnows can ignite great action. Whatever the lure, experiment with different cadences, and don't be afraid to link one up with a lively minnow for a jigged or dead-stick presentation that might be just what that slab crappie is looking for.

PANFISH FIGHTING

The technique for bringing a panfish atop the ice has changed dramatically over the years. Time was, we fished without a reel, battling panfish with jigging rod, light line, and bare hands. How we waged that battle depended on where we were fishing.

If the water was less than 8 or 10 feet deep, one would quickly lift the hand holding the rod, then grab the line near the ice with one's other hand. Then drop the rod tip, hooking it under the line below the handhold, and lift it high again, bringing with it the line. The procedure was repeated until the fish was out of the water. That worked as long as the line was short enough to only require a few loops. Otherwise, it was an invitation for tangles or knots. Part of the fun, we joked.

In deeper waters one was better off setting the hook with a jerk of the rod, lifting it high as before and grabbing the line and then dropping the rod to the ice. With the wind at your back to carry the line away from the hole as you retrieved it, with one hand you'd pull the line through the other hand, close to the ice, keeping the line snug between you and the fish to reduce the odds of the fish getting away. Meanwhile, there was always the risk of line snagging on equipment and ice shards, and tangles and knots often happened. One learned to cut away any knot and retie, or the next fish was sure to be a line-busting tragedy.

No wonder we welcomed rods and reels designed for the ice! There's less finesse and fewer hassles in icing panfish today. Superb small spinning reels and in-line ice-fishing reels make line control a breeze, before, during, and after our panfish encounters.

Species Specifics

The general methods described in this chapter will connect you with winter panfish of all species. But there are subtle differences among them and, if you know that one species inhabits a favorite lake, you should tailor your tackle and tactics to suit it.

For example, bluegills. Likely the best known of the sunfish family of fish, bluegills are also probably the all-time favorite catch of the ice fisher. Flat-sided scrappers, they're an absolute delight on the table. Widespread and prolific, they're willing to gobble almost any bug or grub, natural or plastic.

Generally, you'll find 'gills in waters slightly shallower than those preferred by crappies. And while bluegills (and such closely related sunfish as pumpkinseeds) will on occasion take minnows, grubs of all types are easily the preferred bait.

I know some anglers who fish grubs on plain gold single hooks rather than teardrop or other three-dimensional lures, and they report good luck. Ice flies are also good for bluegills. But day in and day out, it's hard to beat a jig, be it teardrop or other shape, in lead or tungsten, designed to rest vertically or horizontally.

The challenge is that one particular combination of those variables is going to be the best bet for your next fishing trip, and you'll likely have to discover it.

It's for bluegills that serious anglers most often lighten up their line, and since winter bluegills are among the most notorious of light-strikers, it's for them that spring-steel strike indicators are used especially often.

I knew one angler, a bluegill specialist, who used a straight sewing-thread line—no rod, reel, or bobber, wrapping the less-than-1-pound-test line around his finger. He claimed to enjoy a more direct feel of the subtle strike, and he piled panfish on the ice to prove it.

As a general rule, bigger bluegills are found nearer bottom than smaller ones. So if you're catching puny bluegills, try fishing a little deeper, or at least a little closer to bottom.

Sometimes, though, the water's shallow, the bluegills high, and school is in session. One recent late-winter day, when amid a group of several dozen anglers and within a portable shanty that was nearly lightproof, we could see bluegills and their close cousins pumpkinseeds arrive beneath our fishing holes. The water was just 2 feet deep, and these came into view in that narrow space. They'd inspect our baits, sometimes attacking but more often swimming away. Sometimes it was not the studious fish but an interloper that dashed in to snag the bait. Most surprising was how often a bluegill would swim up to a bait, inhale it, and almost instantly spit it out, barely if at all moving the line or strike indicator. Make sure you're watching your line and bobber all the time if you want to ice these fish.

The start-at-bottom rule especially applies to bluegills early in the season. But as winter deepens, the fish seem to move to deeper water and suspend higher above bottom. I once joined a crowd over 30 feet of water and spent far too long fishing near bottom. Several of my neighbors were catching fish, one after another, and I was fishless. Finally I drew some information out of one of them. "They're about three arm-lengths down," he said. I figured that to be about 15 feet deep, and after I'd moved my lure to that range, I started connecting, too. So don't give up on a bluegill hole, especially in midwinter, until you've tried different depths. A flasher or fish-finder can be a great aid in locating them, and a camera can provide positive species ID.

Bluegills are extremely prolific, and in some lakes they're even so numerous they never grow large. Such a stunted population can produce fast action on smallish bluegills. An angler need feel no shame in keeping a mess, although filleting them can be time-consuming.

On bigger bluegills, think about practicing some forbearance: A fisheries biologist friend who loved bluegill fishing released any longer than 9 inches, citing their important role as predators controlling bumper crops of smaller 'gills. He, like me and most of my friends, had

A rod and reel makes icing a crappie from deep water a breeze.

no problem keeping and enjoying 7- and 8-inch bluegills, though, within the daily legal limit, of course.

Crappies come in two brands, white and black crappies. Which you catch depends mainly upon the type of lake in which you're fishing. Throughout much of their collective range, the two species often live in close proximity, sometimes even in the same area of one lake. Even though the two are distinct species and fairly easy to distinguish, most anglers don't bother. Black crappies favor water that is quite clear and supports plenty of vegetation. Brushy underwater areas seem to produce white crappies, especially if the water is murkier. That's probably why they've done so well in lakes built of dammed river water.

Both crappie species depend heavily upon fish life in their diets, although they're more than happy to inhale a wax worm offered through the ice. I've done most of my ice fishing for crappies with wax worms but have seen more than one day when minnows really did the trick. Crappies are also eager feeders at night. Consider spending part of a still winter night on your favorite crappie lake, either in the open or in a shanty. A gas lantern will provide plenty of light, and chances are good crappies will provide plenty of action. (Give safety even more emphasis on a dark lake!)

The crappie has a thin membrane connected to its jaws. That membrane will tear easily if you apply too much force to your line. So be cautious when bringing one up, especially if it feels like a dandy.

Some anglers bad-mouth the taste of crappies, especially those caught in the summer. I've never objected to the taste of a crappie caught in any season, and I've never heard others complain about those extracted from the cold water under a frozen lake top!

MORE PANFISH OPTIONS

Other species will probably figure into your catch. Pumpkinseeds, green sunfish—they're close bluegill relatives and fall for the same gear and tactics. We've iced white bass (which take wax worms and minnows well and provide an exciting under-ice fight), and I've talked to others who mixed rock bass into their bluegill or crappie catch. I've just never met an ice-caught panfish I didn't like!

CHAPTER 8

Society on Ice

A FEW TIMES EACH SEASON, I WALK ONTO A LAKE ON WHICH I CAN SEE no other human beings. That can be an unsettling feeling, something like walking into an empty department store or parking in a deserted lot.

Where is everybody? Is the fishing absolutely dead or, worse, does everyone but me know that the lake is unsafe? Has the Department of Natural Resources closed the lake to fishing, or has the season ended without my noticing?

Usually the emptiness is just a matter of coincidence. Nobody's fishing today, for no good reason, and there's nothing sinister involved.

And for every day you spend on an empty lake, there'll be countless others on which you'll find more than ample company on your favorite body of water.

Coping with the society on the ice can sometimes be as challenging, or as pleasant, as the fishing.

What can you say, after all, when you're fighting a fish on a tip-up, your partner walking the tip-up away from the hole to keep the monofilament in a straight, untangled line, and a snowmobile approaches? There's no sense yelling at the driver, who can't hear through the heavy hood and helmet and is bound to cross the 6-pound test you've been mothering so carefully. In seconds, the line snaps, and you smile weakly and wave.

The tightest form of ice-fishing society is found in a shanty. In these outhouse-sized structures, parties of up to four anglers mix their fortunes

Once word gets around, you're not often lonely when the fish are biting.

next to a heater. The wind howls outside but the anglers are oblivious. Sometimes too oblivious.

One friend tells of a shanty that stood against a harsh north wind on a large lake. The walls shuddered against the wind but held firm.

The base of the shanty, however, hadn't yet formed a tight bond to the ice. As it broke free, the anglers inside poured out of the door, their heaviest coats still inside the coop. And they helplessly watched as their home-away-from-home ice-boated across the lake. One would have been miserable; together, they commiserated their fate and began trudging to shore. I suspected the tale of being apocryphal, until a recent season in which Coast Guard and sheriff staffs had to rescue some Saginaw Bay, Michigan, anglers who were in a shanty that blew loose!

Shanty towns can form. Friends on a large Michigan lake had a bait shop and guiding business, including shanty rentals. Fellow anglers figured Jim and Jeff had a direct line on the fish, and wherever they placed a shanty or two, a village would quickly form, spooking the fish. In Michigan, permanent shelters must bear the name of their owners. The legalities were questionable—I never asked, they never told—but one winter their shanties came out of storage with "Ben Little," the name of a friendly neighbor, on them, and fishing stayed more peaceful.

My friend Jim Lepage anchors his pop-up shelter securely, and then brings out the gas stove, frying pan, eggs, and venison sausage. In no time he's serving biscuit sandwiches, adding a picnic to the ice-fishing memory bank.

We all know that social graces are a key to functioning in a civilized society. Ice fishing is a touch less civilized, and perhaps the society is a little less gracious.

If you ask a gas station attendant for directions, you assume you're being told the truth. But ask an ice angler how they're doing, how they did yesterday, or even what they're using for bait, and it's even money they're fibbing.

"They killed them out here yesterday," one old-timer told me on a small bluegill lake one winter day. "Four guys were out here all morning and they all limited out."

I was one of the four.

We'd gotten skunked.

Kids and dogs are part of the society of ice anglers. For years I fished a spot where you dare not leave a fish on the ice, for a German shepherd was almost always lurking nearby, eager to eat a crappie, run into his

Want company? Serve brunch!

owner's home, throw it up on the carpet, and wag its tail when the owner came out to complain, as if it were our fault!

A friend's Labrador retriever loved three things in life: retrieving downed ducks, stealing fish from ice anglers, and wrapping itself in light monofilament line. He was generally praised for the first, cursed for the last, and forgiven by his red-faced owner for the middle.

Kids are even less predictable. And they're infuriating. They often pay the least attention to the fishing and catch the most fish. They can dress in blue jeans and tennis shoes and stay warm. You can give them the most slipshod tackle and they excel with it. Their first question leads to an interrogation, and they can smell a tall tale a mile off.

A great twist on the challenge of ice fishing is to see how big a whopper of a story you can get a kid to swallow. But do that only if the kid belongs to someone else. If the kid's yours, answer the question in depth. Maybe someday they'll remember your patience, fondly, and take you ice fishing.

CHAPTER 9

Perch: A Special Panfish Case

YEAR-ROUND THE YELLOW PERCH LEADS MANY A STATE'S LIST OF most-often-caught fish. It stands near the top of most lists of the tastiest freshwater fish. Yes, the yellow perch is the angler's friend—and a special pal to the ice angler.

I've caught perch in waters as shallow as 2 feet, through ice nearly that thick. I've also caught them from waters 75 feet deep, while fishing for a deepwater trout. Plenty of perch, too, in between, and caught while fishing for bluegills, crappies, walleyes—and, of course, perch!

Perch just seem to swim everywhere. And every perch, whether from water deep or shallow and whether my fishing target or an unexpected bonus catch, is a welcome addition to my ice-fishing pail. There's little to rival it on the table, with the possible exception of its cousin, the walleye.

And while walleyes and other species are known for moodiness, wariness, or just plain scarceness, the perch can be delightfully simple to catch. Often you need only crude tackle and a rough knowledge of fishing to collect a large bucket filled with perch. But there are also times when even the fanciest trick of the most knowledgeable perch angler fails to produce fish. Most days will offer challenges somewhere between those two extremes.

A closer look at the natural history of perch helps map strategies to catch them.

A perch begins life as one egg in a mass of as many as 50,000, deposited on weeds or brush by the female and fertilized by one or more males nearby. That's the last contact a perch has with its parents. The young are

Many an ice angler's favorite catch: a yellow perch

left to fend for themselves, and they find the world a hostile place. Up to one-half of the fertilized eggs will hatch within a couple of weeks. And for most of the rest of their lives, each of them will be in almost constant demand as dinner, and not just by human anglers. Walleyes, pike, and other perch devour large numbers of small perch. Perch fry, in turn, feed on small zooplankton and insect larvae.

Perch grow quite slowly, reaching 2 to 4 inches of length in their first year of life. At least the 1 in about 5,000 that survives that first year will reach that length. At two years old most perch, in most lakes, will measure about 6 inches long, adding about 1 more inch each year thereafter. But each year, scientists estimate, at least half of the population will be lost to mortality of all kinds.

You'd think that with the long odds facing a perch, they'd be in short supply in most lakes. Actually, the opposite is often the case. Perch tend to overpopulate in many lakes, and that can throw a curve into the growth rates described above. Like the goldfish in the bowl in your living room, perch grow only as large as their environment allows. Put too many perch in a lake, and you end up with a stunted population—a lot of perch of all ages, but short. (Bluegills and crappies, incidentally, exhibit the same tendencies.) Seldom can sportfishing alone remove enough perch to make a real impact, according to biologists, who sometimes are forced even to poison a lake to remove the numerous, too-small perch and allow a more-balanced ecosystem to rebuild.

(A curious situation takes place on Michigan's Saginaw Bay, a lobe of Lake Huron rich in perch-fishing history, both sport and commercial. In the past four decades, a walleye population depleted by overfishing, pollution, and other issues has been restored, phenomenally. Those walleyes thrived on alewives and other prey species, until the food fish vanished amid changing conditions. Walleyes switched to perch, which were reproducing by the millions, and gobbled up all but a few. Those few perch thrived, though, in part by also eating young perch. The upshot is that while fishing rules on walleyes have been loosened, at least in part to boost catches and take the heat off perch, adult perch numbers remain depressed. But where you find them, you can find them big and hungry.

So perch are at a low point—but perch fishing can be splendid. Curious, indeed.)

Many anglers start keeping perch when they've reached a length of about 7 inches. That's when they become noticeably plumper and when filleting yields at least a three-bite slab of meat. In most states and provinces, there's no minimum length for keeping perch, and I've eaten more than a few that were shorter than 7 inches. Cleaning small perch can be a chore, but eating them is still a pleasure. Anglers, including ice anglers, start getting excited when perch stretch to 9 or 10 inches, and foot-long perch are prizes.

Locating Perch

Here's another characteristic of perch that will affect your strategy for catching them: Perch begin life in schools of similar-sized fish and remain a schooling species throughout their lives. Oh, you'll run into a lone ranger now and then, a big perch that swims on its own, but you should keep schools of similar-sized fish in mind. That's both good and bad news for the ice angler. You may have to drill many holes before finding a school of chunky perch. But then, enjoy the often-fast action before they move on.

Early and late ice often find perch in shallower portions of a lake. In midwinter look for them in shallow areas early and late in the day and in deeper pockets in between, haunts similar to those favored by their cousins the walleyes. That's just the general rule, however: On any given day you will likely have to prospect, drilling many holes to first find and then keep up with moving perch action.

A wide variety of lures and baits are used to catch winter perch. Adult perch consume small fish (including other perch), insect larvae and insects, small crayfish, zooplankton, and even snails. And they'll even inhale baits that don't remotely resemble items in that variety-filled diet.

We've worked baits and lures for smaller fish while watching through large (northern pike) spearing holes, snapping to attention when we see the first perch come into view. Bouncing a wax-worm- or wiggler-baited lure off the bottom stirs up a cloud of sediment, and a perch often zips over to take a look, with a little flock of its brethren following suit. A bite and a catch often follows, with repeats if the lure's re-lowered quickly or others are in the water. But before long the school swims off, bringing action to anyone fishing along their line of travel. That's perch fishing most of the time—bursts of action. If they're your primary goal, you'll want to stay on the move, hoping to anticipate their path or intersect that of a new school.

While perch may be seen patrolling anywhere in the lower one-half of the water column, most bites seem to come within a foot or so of bottom, regardless of the water depth. So, keep your lures within that range.

Unlike walleyes, perch seem to hit best at midday, and sun doesn't seem to bother them. That endears them to anglers who like to sleep in and ice-fish during the warmest part of the day.

The hardest thing about perch fishing, again, is doing the legwork required to locate the day's best action. If a hole produces no action in a half hour, you'd best be moving. You may catch fish from the first hole drilled or not until the twenty-fifth. But the action will be worth it once the fish are found. Midwinter perching is always more enjoyable, therefore, if you have a good sharp ice drill or, better yet, a power auger. The new electric augers are a delight!

PRIME PERCH LURES

On big, shallow lakes where cruising schools of perch are common, I still like jigging up perch on Russian Hooks or similar, large-size jigging spoons.

Art Best, who commercialized the Russian Hook, once offered me tips on using these lures, and I paid close attention. "I think colors make quite a difference," Best told me as we watched anglers work perch on Lake Huron's Saginaw Bay in winter. "In my opinion," Best said, "the most consistent fish-catcher is a red-and-white (Russian) hook. Other good color combinations are fluorescent yellow with a red dot, or pearl with a red dot. Sometimes plain copper works best in dark water."

Other anglers swear by pearl in dark or muddy water, silver or bright copper in waters that are clear. Some even carry steel wool to brighten up a metal-finish lure that's lost its luster.

The distinctively elbow-shaped Russian Hook has iced many a winter perch.

But red remains a color common to many popular winter perch baits. Some of my best deep, clear-water perching has come on a far-smaller red teardrop-shaped lure, baited with wax worms or small minnows. Red teardrops easily outfished offerings in other colors.

We've come to rely on Hali-type lures, too, painted lead slabs with single, chain-suspended hooks, for our perch fishing. Baited with a grub or wiggler, the biggest challenge these pose is retrieving the hook swallowed deep by a big, greedy perch! A variety of colors work; the big appeal seems to be the Hali's ability to reach the bottom quickly and kick up a cloud of sediment.

We've also had some splendid perch days bobbing heavy minnow-shaped lures such as the Jigging Rapala or Puppet Minnow, with a grub or minnow head on its central treble hook. These, too, raise an enticing ruckus when bounced on the bottom.

PRODUCTIVE TECHNIQUES

How you fish for perch will depend in large part upon where you fish for them—in deep lakes or shallow waters.

In waters of 8 feet and more, concentrate your search in the bottom couple of feet. You can use spoons, but for deepwater fishing, many perch fans prefer a small ice fly or teardrop-shaped lure baited with a small minnow or grub bait, such as a wax worm or mousie. Wigglers are also good baits.

With panfish-style lures, jiggle the lure slightly, including a slight lift, then let it rest. Watch the rod tip, strike indicator, or bobber, and set the hook when you sense a strike. You may have to delay the set a little if using minnows, to allow the perch to take the bait deeply, but I've lost more fish (and bait) by waiting too long than by setting the hook too soon.

Whatever rig, but especially with minnow-baited lures, keep a tight line and work toward a light touch; for all their occasional ferocity, perch are among the sneakiest of bait-stealing fish. The perch's penchant for bait theft has made popular the use of real or artificial perch eyes for bait. Real perch eyes are the most effective, I believe. Humanely kill the donor fish, insert the hook of a lure into the eye, and smoothly twist the eye out of the socket. Not only are eyes effective as bait, they're virtually indestructible. You can fish for an hour or more without having to change baits. Art Best maintained that the more tattered the eye-bait, the better it worked. He'd fish an eye until there was little left of it.

Best also added to his perch catches by tying a short piece of red yarn so that it extended about a quarter inch on each side of the hook, with the ends frayed. He wasn't sure just what the yarn resembled to a perch, but it's a safe bet it somehow acted lifelike to the fish, known for eating just about anything.

Lure action? Vary it until you find the cadence that produces fish on your specific day. Sometimes perch will nail only lures and baits that are lifted a foot or higher, then allowed to flutter back down. Most takes are on the downswing, so keep your attention riveted to the line. On other days the striped panfish like best a slight wiggle of the lure every few seconds. Sometimes no action is necessary; some of my biggest perch have come not on jigging rods but on stationary tip-ups baited with minnows for walleyes or pike. "Dead sticks," fishing rods left unmoved while another is jigged nearby, are also popular and productive.

Locations? There again, you're going to have to experiment. The shallowest I've ever found perch was in 18 inches of water. The deepest came from 90 feet down.

Some of the best perch fishing in the world is found in fertile waters less than 5 feet deep, especially on big, shallow waters of larger lakes, with a Russian Hook or other large spoon. Begin fishing with a lure baited with a minnow, switching from minnow to perch eyes when you've caught a fish or two. Some anglers use artificial, rubber perch eyes and report almost equal success. The key, simply, is to keep the lure moving and let the spoon's action draw in perch. Hooks of all sizes work well, although when fish are finicky, it helps to jig a large spoon to attract fish and offer a smaller spoon, other lure, or minnow-baited plain hook to the fish in the same hole or one nearby.

Over shallow waters you might want to pinch down the barb of your hook, so you can pull a perch up through the hole, shake it off the hook simply by bouncing the fish's tail on the ice, and re-lower the bait to the productive water in quick, smooth sequence. Try pressing a short piece of rubber band (try red!) onto the hook after the bait. That will dramatically reduce the theft of your bait by the hungry, sneaky perch.

For this shallow-water spoon-jigging, most veterans use rather stout rods wound with heavy line, often 15-pound test or even heavier. Perch just aren't line-shy like other species such as trout, bluegills, and crappies. And just as perch like to follow schools of minnows, northern pike and sometimes walleyes often follow schools of perch, ready for a quick perch dinner. Stouter line offers you better odds of saving your lure and icing a toothy pike or lunker walleye if one can't resist the bouncing, shiny lure.

But perch remain your prime goal. Just keep the lure moving and set the hook when you feel a little extra weight or the *tap-tap-tap* of a feeding perch. Yank the fish atop the ice and get back to business after another. Don't go overboard with the jigging if no action results. Keep the lure moving, but try slowing the pace if the action is slow. Sometimes that works wonders. If not, try a different hole.

Since perch are schooling fish, you want to catch as many as possible before the school moves on to other spots. Happily, the more you catch, the longer the action seems to last. Many perch fans say that as long as food appears available—your bait included—and feeding underway, the perch will remain. Once there's no food nearby, though, they'll continue searching for it elsewhere. That puts a premium on keeping your line in the water as much as possible.

Some serious perch anglers even fish two lines in the same hole, just so that there's always something to hold the perch's hungry interest. That's only practical in shallow water, however.

Another approach is to use a double-lure rigging. One perch-fishing friend ties on a large, shiny spoon a foot or so above a smaller, baited lure. "Most of my fish are caught on the smaller hook," he says, "but the big lure seems to draw them in." He also baits up first with minnows to get the action underway, then switches to perch eyes or other baits that can't be stolen as easily.

Snelled-hook perch or crappie rigs, productive in deepwater settings, can be effective in shallows, too. These offer two plain hooks on separate leaders. A bell sinker anchors the rig to the bottom. Bait each hook with a minnow, wiggler, or grub, and lower the weight. Snug up the line, watch that line, and feel for a tap. It's a good idea to lift the line periodically and allow it to settle back into place. I don't know if a lurking perch thinks its meal is escaping, or if the fluttering minnow draws in perch from afar, but a lot of hits come shortly after a movement of this type. Set the hook before the perch has a chance to steal your bait and escape.

Many perch pros like any method that keeps their success as secret as possible. Often you can work a school of nice-sized perch for a half hour or more, provided that ice-top noise and vibration are kept to a minimum. But if less successful anglers nearby notice that you're collecting a nice mess, they're apt to join you, complete with snowmobiles, power augers, and enough other noise to move the fish to another area. The best perch specialists learn how to catch perch without even their closest fishing neighbors noticing, using a minimum of arm movement to fight their fish, quickly depositing each fish into their bucket with a minimum of fanfare, and generally keeping their good fortune a secret.

If you're not the lucky angler, watch for action nearby. Don't stomp right into a successful angler's fishing grounds, but try moving into the line of travel the perch appear to be following. You might be able to intersect some memorable angling.

Yes, you might be lucky enough to find a school of chunky perch under the first hole you drill, but it's far more likely that you'll have to cut a dozen or more holes and walk across a lot of ice to locate those first keepers, especially over shallow water. And even then, you'll likely want to try a different spot when that school has moved away. I know a few anglers who, having found perch under a couple of holes, will loyally wait for them to return. Often, eventually they will. But few of us have that level of faith and patience. Most of us feel the urge to find our fish instead of waiting for them to find us again.

CHAPTER 10

Making Do

ART BEST ONCE DESCRIBED FOR ME LONG-AGO PERCH FISHING ON SAG-inaw Bay. Best, who most concede first successfully marketed the Russian Hook perch-fishing spoon, wasn't on hand when ice fishing began on that large body of Lake Huron in east-central Lower Michigan; it was millennia old when Euro-American settler culture arrived. But he was able to trace part of the development of the fishery.

When Best arrived on the scene in the early part of the twentieth century, he said the most dedicated and skilled anglers were Russian immigrants who had come to the area to grow and process sugar beets. The bay's abundant yellow perch offered them food and off-hour recreation, especially in winter when many workers were idle.

How'd they catch 'em? It wasn't obvious, Best said. They'd wear coats that hung to their knees or beyond. When they huddled over their fishing holes, these big coats became tentlike screens that hid their efforts. When asked any questions, the immigrants—whether out of jealousy or a language barrier—didn't reply.

Finally, though, the Russians' secret got out. They were using a novel design of fishing lure, and eventually they needed raw materials for making more of them. For scraps of metal, they turned to shops in the sugar factories sprinkled across Michigan's "Thumb" region. Workers in those factories quickly figured out why the Russian guys needed metal—they were hammering out large metal spoons with which they were extracting buckets of Saginaw Bay perch!

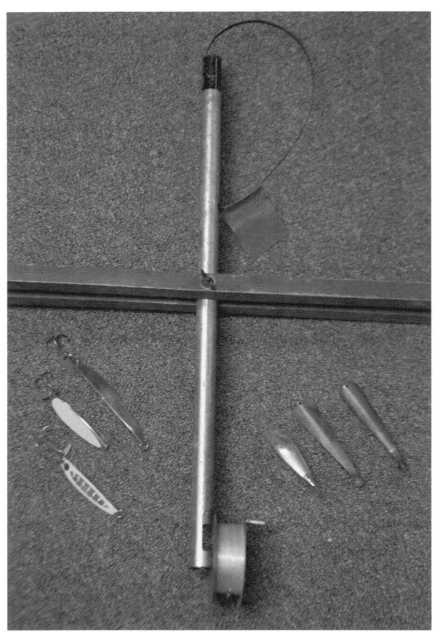

Russian Hooks, right, like the Swedish Pimples at left, and the novel, patented tip-up at center, are examples of grassroots-inspired commercial ice-fishing gear.

Soon Saginaw Bay anglers were pounding out the long, teardrop-shaped lures. Many, following the Russian lead, simply fashioned spoons with the narrow end of the teardrop rounded inward, and the very tip bent slightly outward again to form a rudimentary hook. Others simply soldered onto the spoon shape a regular single-pointed fishhook. Typically, a colored bead—most often red—was installed on the hook bend.

Best said he first saw a Russian Hook in 1936 on a duck-hunting trip from his Wisconsin home to Saginaw Bay. "A fellow gave me a hook and showed me how to use it," he told me in 1978, at the age of 77. "I caught quite a few perch with it and soon began to make a few of them." In the meantime he moved to Detroit for a factory job and soon began marketing his spoons in his spare time.

When the end of World War II made metal widely available again, Best moved to Sebewaing, along Saginaw Bay, and set up full production of his fishing lures. Before he sold his business in 1963, he had opened another plant in Ontario. And in less than three decades, by his best estimates, he sold a million Russian Hooks. The spoons, with the name once trademarked by the Best Tackle Company, are still made by several independent tackle manufacturers and sold by the thousands every winter.

Other, similar success stories could be told of and by dozens of tackle inventors and fishing gear companies: Swedish Pimples (Be de Noc Lure Company), Jigging Rapalas (Normark), Genz Fishing Systems (Clam), and others—their stories mirrored in all types of ice-fishing equipment. For if there's one thing that successful ice anglers consistently exhibit, it's ingenuity. It seems some of the best ice-fishing ideas are hatched on the ice and in the home shop, then brought to market.

Shanty Sourcing

Long before portable, commercially manufactured shelters became popular, ice anglers often prided themselves on shelters—sometimes called shanties, or coops, or bob-houses—they created themselves.

I once met a pair of ice anglers who were unloading a newly constructed shanty from the bed of an old truck they'd driven onto thick ice. The walls of the shanty were made of fourteen old storm doors, taken

Ice-fishing shelters, such as these lined up in a popular smelt-fishing spot in northern Michigan, once exhibited the resourcefulness of their builders!

apart and reassembled in new shapes and dimensions. The base of the structure was the top of a chest freezer. Sheet-metal screws and caulk sealed it all up. Its creators attached a handle at each corner for tie-downs to blocks of two-by-fours slipped through holes in the ice.

That's one example of a hard-wall shanty made from materials others had thrown away. Other shanties—I learned to examine them closely and guess their backstories—have been made from everything from thrown-out crating to insulation material to canvas. And they all work, albeit to varying degrees and for varying durations. (Most shanties are heated. If yours is, make sure to provide ventilation, since carbon monoxide and lack of oxygen kills. Make sure, too, that any insulation is made of a material that won't "gas" you in a fire.)

Catch Your Own Bait

You can "make do" with your own bait, too, especially for panfish.

I like fishing for bluegills and crappies with grub-type baits, and I buy most of them from bait shops. But I've also used grubs cut from the galls of goldenrod stalks at lakeside.

One friend would gather acorns and place them in a pail filled with sand. As the weather cooled, grubs within many acorns bored out of the nuts and burrowed into the sand. A quick sifting and Dale's bait was ready for fishing.

You can cut corn-borers from cornstalks in which you see a hole. Panfish love them. A beekeeper may have a rack overridden by wax worms; if he doesn't ice-fish, he'll probably be more than happy to get rid of them and you'll have a good supply of panfishing baits.

MAKING DO EMOTIONALLY, TOO!

The ice angler's prowess at making do is well known. Now-common pieces of equipment were once the brainchildren of enterprising, frustrated ice anglers toiling in workshops or garages, or even on the ice. Tactics borrowed from open-water angling have been adapted and, I think, improved.

But the ice angler's ingenuity has been overlooked when it comes to the nubbin, the very guts of the homemade: diversion.

No one can promise you fish on every outing. You're going to sit on a frozen lake while absolutely nothing happens. No bites. No tip-up flags. Nothing. Zip. Skunko. Your nose will run, your feet will freeze, and your brain will be only warm enough to entertain doubtful thoughts on the wisdom of your chosen sport.

"I don't have to sit out here and take this," a longtime fishing buddy told me more than once. "Here we are, two grown men, sitting on a block of ice. The wind's blowing, it's snowing to beat the band, and the fish aren't doing anything."

Then, predictably, his face would brighten, a foolish grin stretching from ear to ear. I knew what he was going to say, one more time: "Been fishing all day, expect a bite *any minute*."

Between despair and that "any minute" comes time to fashion some diversion.

On one minus-20°F day, two friends and I sat on pails in the open and watched idle tip-ups on a river impoundment said to contain an abundance of big walleyes and northern pike. It likely still does, but we sure didn't harvest any of them.

After several hours of fishless fishing, our angling egos had become badly bruised. Counseling would have told us we needed to assert our concept of self-worth. And, fortunately, the artistic muses awoke while the angling gods snoozed.

Dale started it, walking away from the center of our tip-up spread through the fresh, deep, untracked snow. We watched as he walked a few steps in one direction, turned around for a few steps, then made a 90-degree shift and walked on. In a few minutes we caught on—Dale was signing his name in the snow, in script, with footprints. Fred quickly followed suit. Eventually, I took my turn. I just nicely got my first name stomped into the snow, however, when I realized both of my buddies had an unfair advantage.

Dale. Fred. Unrelated, but both last-named Smith. Couldn't get names much shorter. I trudged my longer first and last names with a grudge. Before long, one of the tip-up flags flew. Diversion had paid off.

There's no shortage of other ice-top diversions. Try snow-sleeping. On a certain kind of winter day, the sun shines brightly although the temperatures stay cold. The winds stay generously calm. It's cold enough to keep the snow from melting, but the sun's warm enough to remove fears of freezing to death. On those days—and it takes something of a veteran to spot one—you can sleep blissfully for an hour or two. Just make sure your partner's trustworthy—that they'll wake you up if your tip-up's active or they're going home. (Keep the car keys in your pocket.)

Awake, I don't normally go in for the cruel game of trying to set off my partner's tip-ups when they're not looking, faking fish action with a shifty foot or snowball. But if my partner starts the contest, I'm up to the challenge.

I'd rather take on that partner in a rousing game of ice (fishing) hockey. Sorta like regular ice hockey but without puck, sticks, boards, goals, or rules. Just a frozen lake and a chunk of its ice, which you kick back and forth between you until one decides it's been kicked too far to be worth going after. The other athlete wins.

An interesting variation is to keep kicking until the chunk of ice hits one of the tip-ups. This is top-level competition.

We've often thought of ice-fishing diversions too complex for everyday use; we're saving them for desperate times.

Why not try counting the minnows in your minnow bucket? This is a challenging task, especially if the baitfish are small and plentiful. If the fish haven't been biting all day, you probably still have enough minnows to put some sport in this. To get an accurate count, you must devise some way to tell individual minnows apart to make sure you don't count the same one twice. Pick out a characteristic that separates each minnow from its friends. If you want, you can name each.

Counting wax worms isn't much of a challenge, but you might stage a wax-worm race. The little fellows don't move terribly fast. One good race will keep you entertained through the biggest part of an angling day.

You can always play detective. Walk around to other fishing holes, abandoned when their smarter or more frustrated drillers went home to watch the ball game, and try to figure out which was the most productive. Cigar butts, tobacco spittle, and dead bait are among the clues that indicate long-term angling success.

I've found holes with plenty of evidence and decided to try them myself, only to become convinced that it was drilled by a fishless cigar chain-smoker who drooled and dropped minnows onto the ice just to be mean. I've had the feeling, too, that maybe he was watching from shore, choking back a laugh.

CHAPTER 11

Gimme Shelter

It was the perfect place for a portable ice-fishing shelter: an early-February, windswept frozen lake in northwest Lower Michigan.

I don't recall if we were fishing for lake trout, walleyes, perch, or some other species on this single-digit-Fahrenheit day, but I do remember the harsh weather—and I remember the portable shelter.

It arrived in four pieces, pulled on a toboggan behind trudging anglers, each taking a turn. At last, one of the party picked up a cup-style ice auger, the kind long since banished to corners of garages because they were temperamental and hard to sharpen. This one, though, was sharp enough, and he quickly drilled three holes partway into the ice. The holes formed a V, pointed into the wind, each about 2 feet deep and maybe 6 feet apart. He and a buddy set a fencepost in each of them, then added and packed slush and water from another hole to cement them in place. The duo then lashed a tarp to the poles.

And voilà! We had shelter!

The wind blew unabated, but the winter sun and a heater made the lee side a cozy hideout, and I think we even cooked hot dogs in its protection. I don't recall if we caught any fish, and I'm pretty sure we left the posts, perhaps to be used again, when we folded up the tarp. (Littering standards were looser then.)

And I had the first entry in a rich mental scrapbook about ice-fishing shelters.

Yes, we long to get out into the wintry fresh air to enjoy ice fishing—but we cherish protection from the elements, too, and the ability to fish efficiently. Thus the shelter, whether portable or multiday "permanent."

Not that long ago, on any lake, most shelters—tarps, tents, lean-tos, wraparounds, and shanties—were homemade or at least home-designed.

(We call stout, shack-like shelters "shanties" in my Michigan haunts, or "coops." New Hampshire law and angling lore call them by the charming name "bob-houses." They may have a different name on your favorite lake, but they share hard sides and overnight to season-long postings.)

These old-style shanties had good points and drawbacks. Good points? Windproofness and price; they seal up tight and you can build your own. Drawbacks? Weight and maintenance. Lugging them, and periodically prying and propping them up atop slush, and banking them up with snow, is a drag. There are security issues, too: Many shanty owners have learned the hard way not to leave fishing and other gear when they leave, even under lock and key.

Except for spearing, and for some novel fisheries on big lakes such as northern Minnesota's Lake of the Woods, the hard-walled shanty has largely given way to the fabric-walled portable shelter as the face of modern ice fishing. Several companies do make "skid houses," shelters that combine hard walls with lightweight, portable construction, and bridge the gap between fabric portables and heavy hard-wall shacks.

Permanent shanties or coops may appeal to folks who'll be fishing on the same general area of a specific lake through much of the ice season. Such a shelter is always ready, right on the hot spot. Spear-fishers, in particular, like them for their ability to block all light and keep to a minimum ice re-formation over the large spearing hole.

If building your own, make it as windproof as possible, but as in any shanty, make sure there's adequate ventilation so that fumes from whatever heat source you choose can escape. Shanty anglers have died from asphyxiation from fumes from old-style or malfunctioning stoves and heaters; spearers have reportedly passed out, fallen into spearing holes, and drowned.

Many states have laws that apply to shelters left on the ice, especially overnight, including labeling with the owner's name, and requirements that they be removed from the ice (at least each day) by a certain date or when ice becomes unsafe, whichever comes first.

Every year I see more and more portable shelters on the ice, fewer permanent shelters, and a relatively low percentage of anglers fishing in the open. The ease and efficiency of the portable shelter accounts for that.

I recall sitting on a frozen North Dakota lake long ago, next to ice-fishing guru Dave Genz, in one of his early Fish Trap flip-over shelters. I had seen clamshell-like rectangular tents (including the "Clam" made by the company with whom Genz, who many call the founder of modern ice fishing, would ally, the Clam name expanding to grace a wide line of splendid tackle, shelters, and clothing).

Big, perch-rich Devils Lake wasn't yet frozen, but another, smaller local lake was, and it likewise proved generous with perch. Between catches, Genz was explaining the then-novel notion that an ice angler should approach winter fishing as if in summer's bass boat—on a fishing platform that contained and provided everything an angler might want. Like the boat-borne angler, Genz says the ice fisher should move knowledgeably, comfortably—and often. Knowledge comes from portable sonar equipment. Comfort comes from a portable shelter. Mobility is aided with a power auger that makes hole drilling a minor challenge. No longer should one hunker all day over one hole in the ice, or work in a fixed-in-place hard-walled ice shanty from December well into March.

This new premise was embraced most visibly by Genz and Ice Team, a collective of top ice-fishing brands that today includes Clam, Vexilar, Mr. Heater, and several others, refining and promoting this new-age approach to the old sport.

The premise behind Genz's Fish Trap and its industry colleagues is simple. The tublike sleds, with tents that fold over and down over one or several anglers, make it comfortable to sit and fish, but so easy to move that you'll do it often. Decades ago Genz made his own Fish Trap. Soon, with his wife at the sewing machine, he made a few for friends. And before long, lakes throughout the upper Midwest and beyond were sprinkled with the blue shelters that ushered in a new way to ice-fish.

"This is your tackle box," said Genz, in his Fish Trap decked out with boat seats, carpet, and rod holders, tackle neatly stowed and a small

Ice-fishing modernizer Dave Genz, in an early version of his Fish Trap shelter, admires a North Dakota yellow perch.

heater making the space toasty. We'd swiftly bored holes with a power auger, and he now monitored fishing conditions on his Vexilar sounder (whose application to ice fishing he also pioneered with his Genz Blue Box mounting and battery system). As he set the hook on another slab perch, he added, "This is your bass boat. You take it to where the fish are biting." Unlike the gaudy bass boat, though, the opaque portable shelter also shields your success from those who might move too close if they knew how well you were doing.

I couldn't help recalling an even earlier ice-fishing experience I'd had with another industry pioneer, Art Best, on Michigan's Saginaw Bay. He told me about Russian immigrants he and others had observed on the bay, sitting in the open, he said, clad in great coats that protected their bodies from the wind and their tactics from all but frontal snoops. They couldn't—or wouldn't—talk to Best, and he was left to spy as best he could, eventually learning about the lures he'd later manufacture and sell as Russian Hooks. If those potato and sugar beet farmers had been enclosed in a Fish Trap, I mused, their secret might have stayed safe!

Genz and I laughed. This was the hot spot, for this moment, on this lake, this day. Twenty minutes later, though, we were boring more holes. Minutes after that, we were hunkered down in the warm flip-over again, fishing.

"Augering a hole is like making a cast in summer," Genz told me. "If you drill a hole and you don't catch a fish, move and drill another hole. Make another cast. The more holes you drill, the more fish you are going to catch."

Most flip-over shelters on the market today are designed to be towed by snowmobile, quad, or even car or truck, not tugged by hand. (For some shelters, towing brackets, add-on slides, lighting systems, and other add-ons are available.) They can weigh in at 100 pounds and more, a lot to load up alone, and one even needs to make sure they'll fit in the vehicle. I depend so heavily on my pullable shelter that I carry its measurements with me when shopping for a new car. So far, the two-man Fish Trap and the Subaru Forester are a perfect match, and the sled is light enough that I can load, unload, and pull it across the ice alone. But I'll be honest: It's an early model, lighter than today's counterpart. It's

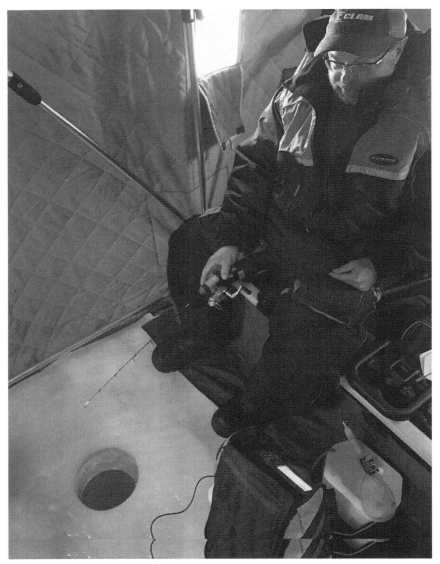

Ice-fishing educator Mark Martin enjoys the comfort of an insulated portable shelter.

easier for me to maneuver, but not as rugged as today's sleds. I've reinforced with fiberglass the corners of the tub several times where they've worn through, dragged across parking lots and rough ice, and it seems as if there's half as much duct tape as canvas on the side walls. Its days are numbered, and, as with a great hunting dog, I'll be sad when I have to put it down. On the bright side, several manufacturers have expanded their lines to include some smaller, lighter flip-overs. Just be sure to consider weight, size, and how you'll move it when shopping for a shelter.

Clamshell shelters remain popular. The founder of the company that would become Clam created its namesake shelter after fishing with an engineer friend. They'd bungeed together a pair of kids' plastic sleds, piling most of their gear on top. "We pulled the whole thing over a snowbank and it tipped—minnow buckets, auger, rods, everything. At the bottom, the two sleds were on top of each other, and the tackle box, embraced by the two sleds, stayed in place." The engineer saw the principle in a shelter that supported a tent and folded like a clam. The entrepreneur saw the market potential. Drawings turned into plans, the pair scraped up the money for a mold, and the Clam brand was born.

Flip-overs and clamshells have been joined on the ice by hub shelters. Like pop-up hunting blinds, these tents are held erect by bowed rods under tension, and are staked down in the corners, often with side guylines added. They make available plenty of space, shake off even harsh winds, and in an ice sled compare favorably in total weight and space with flip-overs. The main difference is agility: With a flip-over, a prospecting ice angler can move from spot to spot easily, while a hub shelter provides a solid base of ice-fishing operations.

Many portable shelters now offer insulated tents. Fire up a heater—and new heater models, with tip-over and low-oxygen protection, are vastly safer than old ones—and peel off your ice-suit parka. Fishing in one of these is as comfortable as fishing in your heated garage would be!

CHAPTER 12

Do You Need—or Want—a Shelter?

OUR 1930S BUNGALOW HOME HAS AN ELEVATED, WIDE PORCH AT THE front and a ground-level patio slab out back. The first encourages open-air interaction with the community; from it we can hail passersby, see what the neighbors are up to, even hear the national anthem sung at a nearby minor league baseball park.

In contrast, the slab in our bush-lined, postage-stamp-size backyard offers a bit of protection from the weather, a touch of privacy, and a more contained spot to focus more intently on whatever subject's at hand.

Together, they seem to provide great metaphors for the two main approaches to ice fishing: traditional, bucket-top open-air ice angling, or its confined-but-comfortable, sheltered cousin, fishing in the portable or permanent shelter.

Each approach has its benefits, each its costs.

My own ice fishing was born on a green, plastic, five-gallon pickle pail, a gear-hauling, fish-stashing, rump-propping man-o'-war. Two pails comprised a setup: a seat and a tackle/fish box.

Bucket-fishing in the open, I learned to keep the wind at my back, and, before switching to rods and reels, to toss hair-thin line up into that wind as I fought fish hand-over-hand, to reduce the risk of tangling. One had to be cautious, lest that fine line catch on jagged ice shards as the line was re-lowered.

My hands would get cold, but they toughened in time, and I could keep tabs on nearby anglers for tips on when and where to move.

Some ice anglers hear the call of the open lake.

Dale, my near-constant partner, would disclose by his body language how he was faring, and I often took cues from him—not just location but cadence, jigging stroke, and, if I were particularly attentive when he brought in a fish—which he did often—how deep to fish.

I could visually eavesdrop on others the same way, tempted to ease my way toward successful anglers in the way that's accepted by ice fishers but rejected by boaters and other open-water anglers.

Back in my bucket days, in brutal conditions it was commonly accepted that you could tuck in the lee of a permanent shanty, or coop, but not a spearing shanty, lest you scare away pike. (If you could not tell the difference, a spearer might well gruffly point it out!)

At day's end it was a simple matter to take the pail, hopefully heavy with fish, in one hand, the hand auger in the other, and trudge off the lake.

My first experience with a portable shelter was a stout-framed rig that rose to support what was essentially a shower stall. It was cozy, but it shuddered in the wind, and its light-sealing bottom flaps were likely to freeze into the slush that invariably developed.

I was soon back on my bucket.

Next came a clamshell coop with fold-up frame. A still-popular design, it met many needs but still required some kind of seat and a bucket or something to carry gear. Sometimes it froze into the slush.

Before long, I was again lugging only the bucket.

Then came Dave Genz's Fish Trap and a host of similar flip-over rigs. They call for a bit of adjustment: shorter rods and tighter hook-sets, for example, to avoid slapping the roof of the shelter; some careful gear layout and hole-drilling planning, to keep fish-finder, heater, camera, and rod-holding pails all within reach and view. But those who like their ice fishing on the run, and keeping the outside outside, quickly came to embrace them. I surely did.

Today, any cluster of portable shanties most likely includes both flip-over and hub shelters, the latter cleverly designed, self-supporting interior-pole devices that pop up easily to provide instant roomy and room-like shelter, even if it takes a little practice—ideally in a controlled, wind-free setting—to master their tear-down and packing. You either carry your hub in a sled or on your shoulder.

The portable shanty shopper should be a weight-watcher. Yes, if you're pulling your rig with a snowmobile or quad, weight really doesn't matter. But if you're on foot, as I almost always am, it matters plenty. It also makes a big difference when you're loading the shelter into or out of your fishing vehicle.

I've swapped out the factory seat in my solo Fish Trap Scout for one that's several pounds lighter, and switched my fish-finder battery for a lighter lithium model. Most recently I've taken on thick ice with Strike-Master's 24-volt lightweight electric power auger and have come to love it. Overall, I've come to place a higher priority on reducing gear—rods, reels, lures, and more—than acquiring more.

But in any shelter you'll find me in front of a small propane heater, quickly shedding heavy outerwear. (Insulated models keep you warmer yet, although this feature adds to weight and cost.)

Sometimes the most satisfying ice-fishing day is one spent immersed in the elements.

In flip-over or hub shelters, there's no ice on your line, and electronics are easy to read, especially underwater cameras.

But to be honest, as snug as fishing is in any portable shelter, and as welcome as that is on days when I want to hide from the elements or the prying eyes of neighbors, there seem to be a few more days every year when I leave the top down on my flip-top, or even abandon it altogether for a pickle pail.

How else would I see the clouds floating in the blue wintry sky, the eagle working the frozen lake top, the cluster of folks forming at the far end of the lake? Even a snowstorm is a cherished scene on an open lake.

I hold fast to memories made in and around permanent shelters, too.

Entering a lightproof spearing coop has always been a magical experience for me, the rectangular hole in the ice a window into the glowing world below as it had been long before underwater cameras offered their own access. Down there weeds draw small fish, small fish attract bigger fish, and once in awhile a fat decoy lures in a big pike at which we might fling a spear.

The ice supports many ironies.

Fishing solo, on a bucket, you can be amid many neighbors but generally alone with your thoughts. Sequestered in a shanty there's intimate society. Stories get told. Tales of heaters gone berserk—at least once kicked, flaming, into the lake.

Don, telling of staring into a spearing hole for long, brain-numbing hours, only to "scream like a little girl" when a swimming muskrat suddenly popped up out of nowhere. He and I nearly broke through the door of a shack when a passing pickup truck—on ice too thin for it—cracked the ice and shot water up through the hole.

Still, more each year, I enjoy joining my open-air neighbors in the shared pursuit of fish and wintry fun.

The privacy of the back deck is fine—but I still love the camaraderie of the front porch!

For those days, I've a quick fix: Lug along the flip-over, and like a freedom-loving teen celebrating summer, leave the top down!

CHAPTER 13

Northern Pike

WHAT HAS MORE TEETH THAN A CROSSCUT SAW? MORE ENTHUSIASM than a ten-year-old on his first fishing trip? More fight than your little brother or sister? It's the northern pike, the big-game species most often identified with ice fishing.

The northern, after all, is no piker. My battered, retired desktop dictionary defines a piker as one "who does things in a small or cheap way." That description just plain misses the northern pike. It's a cool-water eating machine, deceptively slow when it likes, lightning-fast when it prefers. A pike's mouth is filled with teeth that can clutch whatever it attacks. And that's a long list of things, from minnows and worms to mice, ducklings, and even legal-sized gamefish. If what a pike strikes strikes back—the hook hidden within a minnow, for example—the northern's fight is impressive.

There's just nothing a pike does, harking back to the dictionary, that's done in a small or cheap way.

Whether you watch a tip-up and await its red-flag indication of action, jig a shiny lure in hopes of a strike that can slam your knuckles into the ice, or tend a spear inside a dark shanty, you'll end up voting for the northern pike as the prime minister of ice fishing.

The pike is a member of the Esox family of fishes. So, too, are the various muskellunge, several other species of kindred eating machines. There's even a cross between a northern pike and native musky called the tiger musky or "norlunge." Check your state's rules on taking these critters; often there's a larger minimum-size limit on muskellunge, and

Clear black ice sets a dramatic backdrop for this memorable pike catch.

in some areas they can't be kept at all in wintertime. But if the muskies are fair game, follow the same tactics we outline for pike, just upping, perhaps, the size of the baits and strength of tackle to match their bigger size and meaner—if that's possible—disposition.

Any description of a pike must include the tooth-filled mouth, sleek and powerful body, and insatiable appetite. The first two serve the latter. You'll guard against the teeth and power but cater to the appetite.

Pike can be taken by a variety of fishing methods and approaches. You can rather casually set a minnow-loaded tip-up for pike while jigging for crappies or bluegills nearby, or you can pursue the pike vigorously and on its own merits, tending tip-ups or other rigs solely for them. Either way, the northern pike is likely to cooperate. But you can tip the odds further in your favor in several ways.

Pike will eat almost anything, from minnows to gamefish, from worms to ducklings. Stick with baits from the fish family, however— minnows, suckers, and smelt—and you won't go wrong. (A biologist once pointed out that the best baits tend to be longer, slenderer fish— pike-shaped, if you think about it—such as suckers, that go down the pike's gullet easiest.)

TIP-UP TACTICS

Let's talk tip-ups first. I'd guess that more ice-time pike are caught each year on tip-ups than on any other kind of tackle. (As a side bet I'd wager that tip-ups catch more pike than they do any other species, too. The method and fish seem made for each other.)

A tip-up is a device that holds your bait a certain distance off the bottom, keeping a springy flag compressed until the reel turns to release it to an upright position. What turns the reel is the fish you're after.

After that simple description, there are dozens of style variations. Most tip-ups consist of crossed sticks or a plastic platform that lie horizontally and hold the tip-up above the ice. The reel, in vertical or horizontal format, is submerged and is set to engage a wire lever or turn a post if a fish tugs line and turns the reel. That in turn raises a bright-red flag on its springy mast.

I'm fussy about the tip-ups I use for lake and brown trout through the ice, and picky about the ones I use for wary walleyes. But pike just aren't that delicate. They won't automatically drop the bait if they feel resistance, but instead yank it until it comes free. Just about any commercial tip-up made will catch pike. It's what you do with it that counts. Your choice depends mainly upon how much you want to spend, how long you want the tip-up to last, and how many species of fish you want to catch with it.

A relatively new way to fish baits on stationary rigs is the snap-trap, a device that holds a bait in place like a tip-up, but whose trigger mechanism uses rod tension to set the hook, after which the fish can be fought on the rod and its reel. They're a bit cumbersome, maybe, for the walking angler, but they're lots of fun!

Just as with tip-ups, there's an infinite variety of terminal tackle available to the pike fisher. Every serious pike fisher I know is specific about the type of rigging they use. But there's a lot of variation among these tried-and-true setups.

Begin with a length of stout line. Some anglers like black braided nylon line, others gear up with more expensive low-stretch Dacron. Others still wrap on heavy monofilament, and I've even seen tip-ups loaded with sinking fly line. Just make sure you have about 50 yards of good line on the tip-up. And while it's not absolutely necessary to use line so strong, 25-pound test gives plenty of room to apply leverage in a fight. Pike aren't line-shy as are trout and walleyes; wrap on heavier line if you like.

The biggest variation between tip-up pike rigs comes in the last couple of feet of line. To ice these battlers, you have to protect your line against the teeth, and there are a couple of ways to do that.

Traditionally, most pike anglers use a steel leader 6 to 18 inches long. Some braided wire leaders come coated with nylon, some don't, and I don't really see where it makes much difference. The leader most often runs to a snap and a fairly large treble hook, and generally the line carries two or three split shot just above the point where the leader's tied to the main line.

Untold thousands of northern pike have been caught on this protective rigging through the years. And more will continue to be caught. But I can't help thinking there's a better way.

Near my home is a river impoundment known for its early-season panfishing. We can almost always get on the lake before Christmas, once as early as late November. And the bass season here runs through the end of the year. So there's always the temptation to set a tip-up with lighter tackle and a small minnow for bass or walleye, while jigging for panfish with the other lines we're allowed by law.

The double-focus works, but that's not really the point of talking about it here. It just seemed that often when I've rigged up light for bass and walleyes—with 6-pound test line, a small treble hook, and a small minnow—a hungry pike will come along and grab the bait. Maybe six times in ten, I'd coax that pike onto the ice. Two of the other times the fish would somehow escape the hook, and the last two times the line would break against the sharp teeth of the pike.

Now, at this same time of year, some other anglers turn to this same lake for some serious pike fishing, setting their steel-leader-equipped tip-ups and landing a higher percentage of the fish they'd hook.

But I'd have many more flags than them and ice at least as many in a full day's fishing. All while enjoying that much more flag-waving action!

It's commonly accepted that pike aren't line-shy as are some other species. But I think there are times when you'll have better luck by scaling down your tackle. Maybe the pike are spooked a little by a heavy leader. Maybe, too, the difference is in the way your bait acts. Unencumbered by a heavy leader, the minnow can swim more freely, more naturally.

Sometimes, then, you can boost your pike action by forgoing steel leaders. Other days? I remember an outing on the upstream stretches of a large river impoundment where water was shallow and stumps plentiful. Pike were big, too. If you didn't have line of 25 pounds test and a businesslike leader, the pike would take out enough line to wrap you around a stump, leaving you with a broken line and battered spirit.

The friend who guided me to this spot even lost a nice pike when it snapped a heavy steel leader in two. When you tangle with these big,

A tip-up angler watches line peel off at an angle—a sure sign a pike's on the line.

mean fish, some are going to win the fight. That's a big part of the lure of pike fishing after all.

So there's a place, then, for both ends of the spectrum of pike-fishing tackle. If you're going to fish one body of water most of the time, set your tackle up for it—lighter gear if there's plenty of room for fights and pike that run a little small on average, stouter stuff if the lake's cluttered and the pike large.

For focused pike fishing, I now favor a leader of monofilament of about 10 or 15 pounds test, a couple of feet long. Less visible than a steel leader, it's still strong enough to stand some abuse from the fish, provided you take enough care during the fight. And it doesn't matter too much what the backing line is, as long as it's heavy enough to allow you to put some force on the fish. There is a good argument for braided line, since it is easy to handle during a fight and less apt to tangle on the ice. Still, my tip-ups stay wrapped with mono. I've just never had enough problems with it to switch.

Minnow-type baits are best for tip-up fishing. If live bait is available and legal, use it. It has the taste, smell, and look that pike like, and the activity of a struggling bait often bring pike a-running, so to speak. Rig up with a treble hook, and that hook needn't be especially large. I've caught many pike on tiny size 12 trebles and have never had a hook bend open far enough to grant a northern its freedom. Even if you give up a little strength with a smaller hook, rest assured you've made a good bargain on hooking ability. The smaller the point and shaft, the easier it penetrates the hard mouth of a fish.

Golden, blue, and gray shiners are good, especially in sizes of 4 inches and up. Big suckers are the favorite of many trophy pike specialists. And pike often seem to delight in polishing off a live or dead smelt. Pick a hook size to match the size of the bait, but, again, don't be afraid of small, light-wire hooks.

I like hooking live bait just under the dorsal fin. A live bait stays alive and active for long periods, hangs in a natural level position even when inactive, and by the time the bait's halfway down the pike's throat, the hook is firmly in its mouth.

Fishing with live bait isn't always possible, however (or even legal in some states. Your state may require you to add a blade or other attractor to your rigging. Get the rules and read 'em.) Don't despair if you can't use live bait; just bait up with a dead offering. Remember, pike are eating machines; they'll eat just about anything. You can hang a dead minnow in the manner described above, and chances are good a pike will accept your offering. But a friend showed me a method that works better.

That friend uses triangular-shanked hooks known variously as Swedish or Norwegian hooks. They hold a dead bait perfectly level and, when the line's pulled sharply by the angler, the point of the hook pivots, driven home into the roof of the fish's mouth. Rigging is simple. Insert the point through the anal opening of the bait and run it out through the mouth.

If mixing live (treble-hook) and dead (Norwegian-hook) rigs, keep track of which is which. They require different fishing methods. Many pike fans rush to the tip-up when the flag flies, hoping the reel's still turning. They wait for a pause and then strike when a second run begins.

With the dead-bait, Norwegian-hook rig, however, such a wait is neither needed nor desired. No pike is ever going to swallow that big three-sided hook. And you want the fish moving well when you set the hook, since the big point requires more hook-setting force.

My friend walks gently to a tip-up when a flag flies. He waits for the fish to move away from the hole and—wham!—he sets the hook soundly. He wants a quick fight on the shortest line possible, a concession to the stumpy waters in which he fishes. If trying his methods, make sure you don't allow the pike any slack line, since the hook is as much levered into place as it is hooked.

Here's his logic: "A pike doesn't run after taking a minnow in its natural setting. He just moves away a little bit and enjoys his meal. He only runs if he hears or feels you coming. If you're fishing where there are a lot of stumps (which we were), you don't want him to get any farther out than necessary!" So he walks quietly to his tip-up and, as long as the pike is moving, slams the hook home.

Of all the big, dead baits offered to pike, the sucker is probably the most popular. But the smelt may just be the most effective. Veterans swear that the oily smelt gives off some of that oil when resting in the water. And since fish locate their food by smell and taste as well as by sight, pike zero in on this tasty offering. You can catch smelt through the ice on large, cold, deep lakes, keep some frozen in the freezer from the spring runs many areas enjoy, or even buy them dressed in a grocery store. Pike don't care.

Whatever bait you run on your Swedish or Norwegian hook, make sure you set that hook hard. You're driving a large hook through a large baitfish, then into the tough mouth of a pike. It takes a big tug to get the job done.

Another effective approach is the quick-strike rig, a double-hook assembly made with conventional treble or single hooks and wire or heavy fluorocarbon line, and used either with live or dead bait. One hook is placed just ahead of the dorsal fin, the second just ahead of the tail, both just under the skin. The bait rides either horizontally or head-down, determined by the rig's design. There's no need to set the hook with one of these, nor to wait for a pause and second run, and those who use them report astonishing high hook-up rates.

Where do you fish for pike? I've caught them from 3 feet of water and seen them brushing their dorsal fins against the ice in half that depth, and I have friends who've iced them from 90 feet down while fishing for trout. They're a mobile fish, found wherever there's food available. Generally, though, shallower water pays off best. Start fishing near drop-offs and weed beds, where pike have both food and cover available. Pike favor a blend of shallow-water baitfish and cover in the form of vegetation, brush, or deep water. On one fertile and relatively shallow lake, we had a pair of memorable seasons posted along the edge of nearly impenetrable weeds, catching pike that emerged in slow-motion patrol. On a deep, crystal-clear lake an hour away, we watched northerns 16 feet down in 22 feet of water, pursuing prey like fighter planes in a dogfight.

As a general rule, though, I'd start setting tip-ups, as many as the law allows, in waters from 4 to 20 feet deep. And I might not set them all just the way you'd think, down near bottom.

Several expert pike spearers have casually mentioned that they feel many winter pike seekers are missing a good bet. "Did you ever look at a pike's head?" one of them once asked me. "Their eyes look up, not down."

So where do most ice fishermen put their pike bait? Yup, right on bottom or within a foot or two of it. If a pike comes cruising along the bottom, they just might see your bait and take a swipe at it. But if the fish comes in higher than that, looking above him for his next meal, he just might miss your offering completely.

Another friend, one who spends many hours each winter watching from a spearing shanty for pike, said many of the fish he impales are just under the surface of the ice. So that's where he hangs at least some of his tip-up baits. Now I do, too.

Generally, I'm no big fan of gaff hooks for ice fishing. They do come in handy for pike, however. I land fish of most species just by reaching into the hole and cradling the fish's body with my hand and flipping it atop the ice. Sometimes, on a larger fish, I'll grab for a gill cover. But those moves are more difficult and dangerous when you're dealing with a toothy pike. Better to start the fish's head up the hole when it's pooped, then gaff it cleanly and lift it the rest of the way out of the water. Make sure, though, that it's of legal length—that you're not mutilating a fish the law requires you to release unharmed.

Dance a Jig

There's not much that's more satisfying than seeing a tip-up flag fly—unless it's feeling the hammering strike of a big fish slamming a lure. Want to try a different twist on winter pike fishing? Dance a jig.

My first pike on a jigged lure came in open water, and I was fishing for perch. I was attending a meeting near a large, inland lake. Since I hadn't planned on fishing, I was short on tackle but found a casting rod and some shiny silver spoons in the trunk of my car, and with them headed out to the first drop-off to try for perch. Instead, I rowed back in an hour later with a 3-foot-long pike in the bottom of the boat!

I'd guess that most jig-fishing pike fans started in a similar way—catching a big pike while fishing for something else, in open water or on an ice-topped lake. But they stay hooked on jig-caught pike.

Spear-fishermen say a pike moves in to consider a spearing decoy, lurking just offstage and choosing its own moment to move in for the kill. That it does with abandon, and that's the instinct you're counting on as you jig for a northern. It helps to always imagine that deliberating predator just out of sight.

Jigging has several advantages. It's mobile, for one; you can quickly work a half dozen holes or more. It's also active. And, most dramatically, you're on a direct hook-up to a close-in pike.

Gear up with an outfit that lets you pay out line. Use a reel-equipped ice-fishing jig outfit, or a short casting rod and reel. Forget steel leaders; they hamper the action of your lure. Many lures take pike through the ice, the best known perhaps Swedish Pimples and jigging-model Rapalas. But don't hesitate to try the spoons so successful on pike in the open-water months, the red-and-white Dardevle tops among them.

Line should test about 15 pounds. Any less and you risk breaking off the fish at the hook-set; any stronger and it will cut the action of the lure.

Pike seem especially apt to strike a lure when it's lying at rest between jigging motions. So let the lure pause occasionally. But otherwise keep varying the cadence, force, and depth at which you jig the lure. Cover all depths patiently before moving on to another hole.

Jig-caught pike do strike hard. We sat on an impoundment watching tip-ups one sunny winter day, and the discussion turned to jigging. Two of us had caught some nice lake trout a few days earlier by bouncing spoons off the bottom. Finally one of my partners pulled a tip-up (to stay within the legal number of lines allowed), grabbed a jigging rod, and began bouncing a Dardevle off the bottom 4 feet beneath him. He and the 2-foot-plus pike were equally surprised at the strike a few minutes later. The fight was brief on the short line, but the effect was lasting; all three of us cheered the action of jigging for pike.

Try to stay ready for a strike. But I've a strong hunch, the result of pleasant experience, that you'll get a smashing strike when you least expect it.

The northern pike—teeth, muscles, and appetite—is a mean customer. You can test his prowling hunger with a tip-up or challenge him to a brawl on a jigging rod. Either way, he's ready for action. You'd better be, too!

CHAPTER 14

Spearing

WANT THE BEST OF FISHING AND HUNTING COMBINED? YOU JUST MIGHT find it in what's called a darkhouse, spear in hand!

The best-known quarry of the winter spear-fisher is the northern pike, and many are the pike impaled upon spear tines each winter across the ice region, their captors opening the door of a warm, dark shanty to toss the trophies onto the sunlit ice. (Traditional spearing coops are hard-sided; some spearers use portable, soft-sided shelters, and manufacturers have brought to market models designed specifically for spearing.)

Hunger is the pike's undoing. The spearer usually hangs a decoy—either a live sucker 6 inches long to twice that length or an artificial replica of a game or food fish.

(I've got a bunch of old fishing tackle—stuff I really treasure—and my favorites are a half dozen old spearing decoys that some industrious angler carved from driftwood, adding lead weight in hollows, aluminum fins, and primitive paint. You can tell the alleged brook trout from the likely sucker, but the fact that both worked reduces my fear of failing at spearing because of a faulty decoy! Proof of that is a deke my then-pre-school daughter and I carved; it drew a fish its first time down!)

Spearers who use a live fish as a decoy report one big advantage. They say that an active sucker—which they'll use for several days if possible—will "freeze" when a northern comes on the scene, allowing the angler to ready his spear even before the pike comes into view. It's a three-way war of nerves among the northern, the decoy, and the angler. My old spearing

Patience pays off in a pike for this spearer.

partner would confide in his decoy, "I'm the best friend you have," ready to spear the decoy's would-be assailant.

To an observer, spearing might seem casual—waiting comfortably in a dark shanty until a pike appears below, then impaling it with a spear. But there's far more to it than that: You've got to be a knowledgeable, patient, and alert angler to succeed at this sport.

The first requirement for successful spearing is darkness. Your illumination comes from the lake below. Pike are active almost exclusively in the daytime, so it's up to you to make sure your fishing shanty is light-proof. Every window must be covered and every seam and corner sealed. Make sure your stove, if you have one, doesn't throw any light.

(Make sure, though, that while keeping the light out, your shanty provides good ventilation. Don't give oxygen loss or carbon monoxide a chance to end your life.)

Your spearing coop must also be quiet. Get surplus gear out of the way, where you won't be banging it around. A piece of old carpet on the floor of a hard-sided shanty can cut noise further. Old-time spearers even advise newcomers to the sport to wear dark-colored clothes. Do everything you can to ensure that you'll see the pike and it won't see you.

Each spearer has their own favorite spear design. Here, though, are some general guidelines. Make it a weighted spear so you don't have to throw it too hard, letting gravity give your toss a boost. Make sure it has from seven to nine tines and is about 7 feet long. You'll want a rope attached to it, too, especially if the water's deeper than the spear handle is long.

On one lake on which we spear for pike, the best waters are 18 feet deep. We install handles nearly that long on our spears so as to lower them in advance—and when we raise them, poke the handle through a hole in the shanty roof!

For standard-length spears, here's a rope-rigging tip from the Michigan Department of Natural Resources: "Run your rope through a cotter-pin on the spear's handle down to the tines where it is tied fast or secured with a metal ring. When you hit the mark and start to haul the fish in, a slight jerk pulls the cotter-pin out and lets you lift the spear with

A medium-size northern pike, left, eyes a large sucker decoy.

the tines up. If the fish is not speared very well, this helps to keep it on the tines instead of giving it a chance to work free!"

Other tricks can help, like keeping the spear's tines just underwater at all times, or at least slipping them in prior to tossing the spear. If you throw it in one movement from above the water, the pop and splash may well send the pike on its way before the spear gets to it.

Maybe the hardest thing about spear fishing is cutting the hole through which you watch for the fish. An auger cuts round holes, not rectangular ones, although it can drill starter, corner holes. From there, go to work with a hand saw (modern or antique—mine's a hundred years old and was used to commercially harvest Mississippi River ice!), spud, axe, or chain saw. In a pinch, you can connect a rectangular series of auger holes, but it's sloppy work. And of course, as the winter fishing season lengthens, the task of hole-cutting gets tougher.

The start of each day usually requires chipping away a skin of new-formed ice. Make sure you have a spud and a long-handled skimmer for clearing the hole.

Mark spearing holes when you leave. In my part of the country, a branch or piece of brush stuck in the snow is a universal signal of an abandoned fishing hole, and we stay clear. Leaving an unmarked spearing hole can have tragic consequences for an angler, skater, or snowmobiler coming along later. Mark it well, even if it requires a long hike to shore for a suitable marker. It's a major responsibility, and a small price to pay for the pleasure of tending a spearing hole.

Pike aren't the only target of the spear, either. In many states muskellunge are legal quarry, and the same tactics take them as are used for pike. An unusual through-ice spear fishery for yellow perch takes place on Michigan waters of Lake St. Clair. And then there's spearing a creature that can be 6 feet long and weigh 200 pounds—a lake sturgeon!

SPEAR A STURGEON?

Sturgeon spearing is both unusual and limited, taking place only on designated lakes and during special seasons. Your best bet may be to hire the services of a guide on one of those lakes; they will supply the gear as well as the know-how and local knowledge. At least consider renting a shanty already in place over productive sturgeon-spearing grounds.

These behemoths, often weighing in at more than 100 pounds, call for specialized tackle and techniques. And since they're relatively scarce, you need to spend your hours and days over areas regularly used by these prehistoric-appearing fish.

The most popular sturgeon-spearing approach is to lower a wooden, plastic, or metal decoy into water about 20 feet deep, then wait for curiosity to bring the big fish into spearing range. The decoy, apparently, doesn't resemble anything in the fish's diet, since sturgeon feed mainly on the larval stage of mayflies called wigglers, on fingernail clams, crayfish, and some aquatic plants. A fish biologist told me they have no provisions for chewing food.

Don't expect to see a "normal-looking" fish swim into view when you're huddled in a sturgeon-spearing shanty. Physically, biologists say,

A pair of anglers, a pair of spears, and a sturgeon on the ice

the sturgeon is a holdover from prehistoric times and is believed to have evolved about a hundred million years ago. It has a big, sharklike tail, bony body, and long, rubbery snout from which feelers suspend—all in all, one of the strangest sights an angler can view.

(Nearly as odd-looking is the gar, a long, spear-shaped fish that often swims in the same areas; one coasted into view as I sat in a lightproof shanty on northern Michigan's Black Lake, and I was nearly as surprised and pleased as if it had been the sturgeon for which I was hoping. There's no spearing of gar; it swam on.)

Sturgeon meat is said to be excellent when smoked or fried, their eggs can be used as caviar, and even their bladders can be made into a pure form of gelatin used in jellies.

The sturgeon now receives far more respect than it did a century and a half ago when commercial fishermen on the Great Lakes cursed the big net-wreckers. Thousands of sturgeon, according to published reports, were stacked on beaches, dried, and burned.

Today, thousands of anglers gather on the ice of Black Lake, where a special season runs until a set and small number—lately six or seven, and met in less than an hour—of sturgeon are iced. It's a closely monitored and highly celebrated event, which spotlights the efforts of the conservation group Sturgeon for Tomorrow and others to protect and enhance the sturgeon population.

Neighboring Wisconsin's massive Lake Winnebago, with a larger sturgeon population, draws an even larger number of spearers, with a popular festival of its own. The sturgeon-spearing season there stretches sixteen days, unless a conservation-minded harvest limit is reached first.

CHAPTER 15

Walleyes

WHEN WE PARKED OUR PICKUP TRUCK AT THE END OF A SNOW-FILLED logging road just before dawn one morning, one car was already there, and its frosted windshield said it had been there for at least a few hours. Maybe abandoned, we thought.

We gathered our pike-fishing gear from the back of the truck, silently congratulating ourselves on getting up so early and getting a really early start on our day's fishing, but we were puzzled by the other car.

The first rays of sunlight were just starting to trace multicolored fingers in the sky when the bright beam of a gas lantern bobbed over the top of the high riverbank down which we planned to walk to a little-known (or so we thought) pike hot spot.

Two fishermen appeared, one carrying the lantern and the other lugging a plastic pail packed with tip-ups, jigging rods, and fish. The tails of three fish stuck out from the bucket; they looked like 18-inchers, anyway, a white spot on each tail.

"How'd you do?" our surprised fishing host asked the anglers. "Got a few walleyes," came the response; the speaker seemed disappointed that we'd already seen their fish. He unlocked the back of the frost-covered station wagon, and his partner quickly stashed the bucket in the car, without letting us check out the catch. They fired up the car, scraped just enough frost off the glass to see, and rumbled away.

"That's walleye fishermen for you," our pike-fishing host muttered. "They can be downright anti-social."

When walleyes are located, the action can be impressive—as will be the eating!

Maybe, but then again maybe they're just careful and guarded. It takes more planning, effort, patience, and luck to catch walleyes than just about any other ice-fishing target, but their elusive nature and gourmet flavor combine to make all that worthwhile. That doesn't mean you need to tell everyone about it!

Walleyes are seemingly the ultimate quarry of the ice angler. They're distributed about as widely as pike. They school like perch and resemble those striped cousins in their strong preference for a fish diet. But they're also as wary as brown trout. And no fish can top them for taste on the table. When ice-fishing prizes are compared, the walleye is almost always accorded first place.

Serious walleye anglers often beat the sun to their favorite spots, and they or others like them sometimes watch tip-ups against a sunset background, too. Even night fishing's a thing. Unlike panfish, trout, and even pike fans, who are fairly gregarious, when walleye fishers find a hot spot—like the backwater bayou on which we planned to catch pike in the sketch above—they try to keep it to themselves.

Does that challenge appeal to you—trying for a wary, wandering fish that requires both delicacy and persistence? Maybe even a bit of subterfuge? And pays it back with a memorable meal? Then the walleye's your fish.

I first learned walleye patience on a big inland lake, where I'd joined a fish biologist for an evening outing. He'd promised to teach me how to connect with walleyes and warned me in midafternoon that it might be dark before our efforts paid off.

Sure enough, the couple of daylight hours remaining when we reached our fishing spot a mile or so offshore brought us fishing action—but only on small northern pike and a perch or two. Meanwhile we fine-tuned our tackle and tactics and fueled our enthusiasm.

Two basic approaches catch most midwinter walleyes. Jigging a light line baited with a lure, live bait, or both, is always a good way to connect. Watching a lightly set tip-up baited with a small minnow on light line is another.

When Jerry finally showed us some walleye catching, it was on a rig that combined the best of both worlds. His "tip-down" comprised a short spinning rod held in a cradle, with a little clip to hold the line at the base of the stand. The bail of the open-face spinning reel was left open, the line held in the clip, and the rod set with its tip pointing slightly more up than down. The bait was a 2-inch minnow impaled on a small treble hook, with just enough weight added to hold the minnow down.

On such a tip-down rig, it takes just a little pressure for the fish to pull the rod to a position below horizontal, tug the line from the clip, and then peel line freely from the reel. The angler is then free to lift the rod out of the holder and fight the fish on it and its reel, just as the jigging angler would.

"Here we go," Jerry shouted, as the sun dropped behind the western shore of this big lake and a nearby rig finally tipped down. Jerry fought the walleye several minutes as full darkness fell, and then eased the 17-incher through the ice. "That's all there is to it!"

Of course, there's more than that to catching walleyes in the winter. You have to understand these fish. You have to remember their tendency to feed in low-light periods—dusk and daybreak and, often, in the night-time in between. You have to track their movements through the season and, even more precisely, through the day, as they move from cover to feeding zones and back again. You must scale down your gear for these wary fish. And most of all, you must have the patience required to wait for them.

As Jerry said, with a laugh, that's all there is to it.

Walleye will sometimes give you a big head when your favorite warm- or cool-water lake first freezes over. Then 'eyes, like most other fish, are more active than they'll be for the rest of the winter, eating whatever they find, at just about any hour of the day. Often food species such as emerald shiner minnows move toward shallows and shore, with hungry walleyes right behind them. You can get spoiled, and sloppy. About the time you do, midwinter sets in. And that season is not a forgiving one. You've got to do everything right.

Of all the variables that affect ice fishing for walleyes, time of day is one of the more crucial. All-night fishing doesn't really get too many takers; most anglers rate the two hours on either side of sunset and the two either side of daybreak as best.

An insulated portable shanty was the scene of this walleye catch.

That's when you want to be bouncing a jig or spoon—Swedish Pimple or Do-Jigger, maybe, or Jigging Rapala or Puppet Minnow—just above bottom. (Size 5 in any of those lures is a favorite.) You can run a straight line to the lure, or attach a 3-foot-long leader of about 8-pound test monofilament or fluorocarbon. Many anglers use a swivel or snap swivel to allow the lure maximum action while avoiding line twist. Fish 1 to 2 feet off the bottom to start with, and try quick jerks of the lure. (An underwater camera can help you learn how your chosen lure behaves, or you can give it some test tugs just below the surface.) Make your lure look like a frantic or wounded minnow. To cash in on the walleye's preference for fish, add a dead minnow, the tail or head of a minnow, or even a flap of skin cut from a fish to the lure.

Like their perch cousins, walleyes also tend to travel in schools, though usually not in the tight packs in which perch are found. Don't be surprised if you mix perch or pike into your catch, though; some of the best walleye catches I've seen were part of mixed bags.

One walleye expert on big, walleye-rich Houghton Lake in northern Michigan told me some of his best tip-up catches came in full darkness. His rigs feature light line and small hooks, and he sets his tip-ups close enough to him that, even in the dark, he can scoot to the tip-up and set the hook before the fish can drop the bait.

(You can buy tip-ups equipped with lights that illuminate when the flag is tripped, or add these or even alarm sounders as accessories.)

Tip-up fishing anglers often connect when it's still light, too, especially if they've scaled their line down to around 4 pounds test and chosen tip-ups that release easily and smoothly. Less-expensive rigs, often with small, metal reels, may be OK for pike fishing, but I don't use them for skittish walleyes. A larger reel requires less pressure to release the flag, and its smoother action makes it less likely the fish will spook as it takes the bait. I tie on light-wire treble hooks in size 10 or 12, and clamp on only enough shot to keep the bait down; one small split shot is often all that's required for the 1½- to 2-inch minnows I prefer.

One rigging variation is running the main line through a small, egg-type sinker, then tying it to a barrel swivel. Add a leader 2 or 3 feet long running to the small treble hook. When a fish hits, the sinker falls to the bottom and the line feeds smoothly through it. As a result the fish can take out line without feeling much resistance.

Walleyes hug bottom, so you'll want a clip-on weight for checking the depth and adjusting your line before adding a tiny clip-on bobber at a point a few inches beneath the reel. When your flag is tripped, the bobber helps you tell if there's a fish on the line, since a false release will leave the float within view. Whether the waving flag results in a fish or not, the bobber makes it easy to reset the rig at the same depth.

Want an argument? Ask two walleye anglers when to set the hook. One will probably warn you never to yank the hook home until the fish has made one run, paused to swallow the bait and hook, and begun another run. The other will likely swear that the small hook will engage, in the jaw, as soon as the flag goes off. I've seen plenty of fish landed (and lost) each way. It's up to you.

There's less disagreement on the best places to find winter walleyes. Mainly fish-eaters, their food supplies are the weed beds and shallows of warm- and cool-water lakes, although they like spending nonfeeding daytimes in deeper, clearer waters in either lake type. You'll want to intercept them between the two areas. Many anglers know from summer and winter experience where main weed beds are located within a lake.

We once pinpointed top spots by selecting several landmarks and noting how they lined up from the location to which we wanted to return. Now, we most often use Global Positioning System (GPS) navigation, in stand-alone hand-held units or incorporated in fish-finders, to return to favorite spots. If you're new to a lake, try to find a map showing weed beds, or coax the info out of an old-timer on the lake or in a bait shop. Better bet? Learn to use your sonar to detect weeds, or drop an underwater camera down test holes to assess the cover below.

Walleyes are big fans of bottom structure, cover, or any change in the contour of the bottom. Rocky points, reefs, and other sharp drop-offs are probably the best-known of "classic" walleye hot spots. But structure can be far more subtle. On one large, flat bay I know, a rise of even just a foot above surrounding bottom can be a walleye magnet.

If you can figure out both ends of the walleye's movement pattern— the deeper water in which it spends most of its day and the food supplies to which it turns at evening and daybreak—try working several locations between the two. Set as many tip-ups as your state allows, and spread your angling party along the daily migration route. If one person seems to be getting more than their share of the action, sidle on over.

But do so quietly. Walleyes aren't bold, and it takes a quiet, light-weight approach to fool these fish. They're worth the effort though—both flopping on the ice in the rays of a fading sun or lantern and popping in grease on a hot stove.

Chapter 16

100 Degrees of Difference

Sometimes the key to enjoying the great outdoors, such as ice fishing for walleyes and saugers on immense, frozen Lake of the Woods at Baudette, Minnesota, on the US/Canada border, is keeping that outdoors outdoors.

Maybe it's towing a travel-trailer called a wheelhouse that, once on the ice, hunkers down to become a sumptuous ice shanty. These deluxe portable fishing cabins have price tags like new cars.

Or maybe it's coughing up about a hundred-fifty bucks each to rent a bunk-equipped sleeper shanty in which to play cards, cook a meal, catch some z's, and, yes, fish, as the spirit moves one.

For a handful of us outdoor media types, on two dramatically subzero days (25°F below at each daybreak), it meant terrestrial sleeping in snug cabins at River Bend Resort, relaxing and refueling in its bar & grill, and days between early breakfast and late dinner spent in cozy rental fishing coops owned by the resort and tended by guides.

For some reason walleyes here are especially active from 9 to 5, not the low-light periods best known for walleye fishing in other locations. This big lake is famous, in fact, for its walleyes and their close relative, saugers, and for their novel habit of baiting best in full daylight.

"There's no night bite here," said guide Alex Peterson, as he showed us around a shanty roomy enough to fish six or more, heated around the clock by an LP furnace so its fishing holes don't refreeze.

Spacious and cozy, even at minus-20-something degrees, this rental fishing coop is on Lake of the Woods.

We'd followed Peterson in our own vehicles across the "ice road" marked and maintained by River Bend, as were other roads by other resorts and guide services. The ice, by the way, was more than 2 feet thick.

Brandi Johnson, who with her husband, Paul, has owned River Bend for eleven years, explained that each local resort fishes its own area on the lake, respecting the zones claimed by others, sometimes decades ago. There's no real ownership of these public waters, of course, and no way to restrict the fishing public. Still, anglers purchase from local shops or are issued by resorts "ice-road permits," which support the work of keeping access open. (Several times we'd see big pickup trucks driving massive plows through the ever-shifting snow cover, sending plumes high in the air.)

Several miles offshore, in River Bend's zone, we were soon tending lines in the coop's more than a dozen holes, staring at fish-finder screens (some resort-provided, some our own), watching our lures. Some of us

Sid Dobrin, Florida-based "Fishing Professor" podcaster and English professor, shows his first ice-caught walleye.

were testing Live Target Sonic Shads, Flutter Shad, and Rattlebaits to which we added a fathead minnow to one of two hooks; fish loved them.

We caught walleyes and even more of their sauger cousins. For walleyes there's no minimum length here, but fish between 19½ and 28 inches must be released unharmed. One trophy walleye of over 28 inches can be retained (or could be; we caught none that large) as part of the daily combined limit of six walleyes or saugers, no more than four of them walleyes. We collected the under 19½-inch makings of a great fish fry for later.

I had dressed for the subzero outdoors the first day but, confident now in transportation, guide, furnace, etc., and sure I'd be doing all my fishing indoors, downscaled dramatically the second.

One couldn't miss the contrast between indoors and out: Each time the door opened, such as for someone's brisk hike to an on-ice outhouse, clouds of steam rolled in.

From one steam cloud emerged guide Peterson with a stack of hot pizzas pre-ordered from the lodge for midday delivery! Arranging such a treat was just one subject explained by posters on the coop's interior wall, along with fishing regulations, lake-top etiquette, social media posting tips, and more.

We only caught a couple of walleyes that required measuring to make sure they weren't in the protected slot, at its small end. In the main these are not massive Saginaw Bay or Lake Erie walleyes or outsized saugers. But fillets of these relatives of yellow perch, in big-perch sizes, are exquisite. River Bend proved that with our catches delicately battered and fried as appetizers two nights in a row.

Three fish fries, in fact. Caroline and Oliver Taylor had shared their catch at dinner the night before our fishing began. They'd come up from their Jupiter, Florida, home after fifteen-year-old fishing-crazy Oliver had stumbled across ice fishing in internet videos. His airline pilot mother booked an adventure they had both loved and already planned to repeat.

Some in our crew, mostly northerners, said the Taylors' pattern made good sense, grabbing a short reprieve from mild Florida weather by

A "wheelhouse" towable fishing cabin on a northern Minnesota highway

coming up north, instead of the northerners' typical and too-temporary break from winter realized by heading south for a few days.

But this lake's ice anglers are committed. On the five-hour drive north from Minneapolis, we had seen at least 200 wheelhouses, trailer/fishing shanty hybrids, being towed south at weekend's end, almost all behind big, ballsy pickup trucks. These are portable fishing cabins, often decked out with couches and chairs, tables and beds, cooking fixtures, porta-potties. Not hard to get $70,000 tied up in one, it's said. But winter here in northern Minnesota is long and cold; you can stretch your wheelhouse investment across many fishing days.

Brandi Johnson said wheelhouses have become the rage on Lake of the Woods within the last decade, goosed by the COVID pandemic and its push toward outdoor recreation.

"Lots of resorts dislike them," she said. "They say [wheelhouses] are using our roads and so on. But we love them. We want people to enjoy the lake. These are not our fish." Johnson added that local folks do rightly grumble about any trash left behind.

Our guide Alex Peterson said he'd once owned his own wheelhouse. "It's a lot of fun. But it is funny how easy it is to get help setting one up, and when it's time to take it off the ice and put it away, everyone's gone," he said with a smile.

Of those who elect to rent shanties, I asked Brandi Johnson, who's the winter customer at Lake of the Woods?

"It's changed a lot," she said. "It used to be outdoorsmen, hard-core fishermen. Now it's more families, lots more women. We get a lot of people who have never ice-fished. They want to fish, but it's not about being in a crowd."

Some winter anglers are drawn to a rented, bunk-bed-equipped sleeper coop, Johnson said, a bucket-list thing. "People want to try it. You either love it or you dislike it. It's ice camping." On the ice around the clock, "you can sit and play cards, watch the game or a movie on TV, and still be fishing." Special rigs suspend baits, revolving to ring a bell if there's a bite and summon a distracted or sleeping angler.

"The average [sleeper] stay is two or three nights. After that, you miss the amenities" of onshore living, Johnson said. But the resort's newest sleepers have both TVs and stoves. "You can make pizza or put a lasagna in the oven. You can cook your catch—although you have to do it in a certain way, and count those fish toward your limit." For the TV you can rent a generator or bring your own. With a smartphone personal hot spot, you can access the internet.

To fish like we did, sleeping in River Bend cabins and fishing in its coops, budget about $220 per person per night and fishing day, with discounts for midweek and longer stays; meal packages are also available.

Partway through our first fishing day, I did some other math:

Seventy-something degrees in the shanty.

More than 25-below outside.

Yeah, you're experiencing a difference of roughly 100 degrees.

That and the willingness of tasty walleyes and saugers to smack baits and lures made a strong argument for enjoying the outdoors—by keeping it outdoors.

CHAPTER 17

Trout

MANY TROUT ANGLERS EQUATE TROUT WITH SUMMER. THESE FOLKS love to cast dry flies and swat mosquitoes, and come cold weather they retreat to tying benches and fishing tackle catalogs and mark time until the following spring. Sadly, they miss out on some of the very best of trout fishing: ice fishing for trout.

From the vast Great Lakes to idyllic inland trout lakes, fishing for minnow-chasing marauders or depth-plumbing opportunists, chugging heavy lures on stout sticks or dancing tiny ice flies on wispy line, you can catch any species of trout through the ice and have a superb time doing it.

The first step is settling upon a quarry. On some lakes that's no problem, since the lake may offer only brown, rainbow, lake, or brook trout. But many lakes are home to several kinds of trout. One of my favorites offers three trout species, plus a hybrid trout, and a salmon that's a close relative of the brown. There, you must adapt your tactics to fish you seek, but that's part of the fun.

This beloved lake holds good numbers of wide-ranging rainbow trout, plus brown and lake trout, species that differ greatly in their habits and habitat. It's also home to some splake, a hybrid cross between lake trout and brook trout. To confuse the picture further, the lake has also received periodic plants of landlocked Atlantic salmon, closely related to the brown trout.

The name "trout" throws us off. Lake and brook trout are members of the char genus. Rainbow trout are now considered part of the Pacific

A massive lake trout like this is the trophy of a lifetime.

salmon genus. And brown trout and Atlantic salmon are their own closest relatives. Still, we call all but the Atlantic salmon "trout."

Enough science for now; let's catch 'em and worry about formal IDs
another time.

Ice fishing's an effective approach to any of the so-called trout species, so much so that special rules in force in many areas and on many
lakes restrict the methods, bait, minimum size, and daily catch.

LAKE TROUT

Deep-dwelling lake trout have long been favorites of ice anglers, both on
the big Great Lakes waters in which they're native and the far-flung lakes
in which they've been introduced.

Two types of tactics take ice-time lake trout best. The first is the
tip-up, a crossed stick or plastic platform that suspends an underwater
reel that holds your line and bait at a certain depth. When the fish takes
the bait, the reel turns, releasing a flag that summons you to action. There
are many designs of tip-ups, from plain inexpensive models to some that
flash lights, work on adjustable magnetic systems, or bob the bait in a
wind-powered jigging motion. Any will catch lakers, provided their reels
are large enough to hold the line needed for fishing in deep water and
battling what can be big, long-running fish.

For all-round trout fishing, I spool up monofilament line of 6 or
8 pounds test on a tip-up equipped with a large reel that holds plenty
of line and releases smoothly. For lakers I run that line through an egg
sinker and tie it to a barrel swivel. To the barrel swivel I tie a leader
2 pounds test lighter than the main line, 2 or 3 feet long. The leader
runs to a light-wire hook of about size 10 or 12. Bait up with a blue or
gray minnow or live smelt and fish just off bottom in waters 60 feet or
deeper for lake trout and splake, the latter of which behaves much like
its half-parent laker.

The most challenging part of winter lake trout fishing is finding the
fish. Once you do, they're usually willing to take practically any living or
dead minnow or fish bait.

Within your party, stretch the legal number of tip-ups over as wide
a range of depths and structure as possible, in hopes of determining a

winning pattern for that day. But at least lakers stay near bottom, which removes another question mark from the angler's mind!

You've a choice of several live baits when setting tip-ups for winter lake trout. Smelt make up a big part of their diets; if you can find them or catch them, they're deadly on lakers. Blue and gray minnows are good, too, while I've had little luck on golden shiners. Some laker fans catch big ciscoes and lay them, dead, on the bottom, as lake trout bait. They ice a few 20-pound scavengers each winter.

How well do smelt work? We've made special trips to a lake 50 miles from home the night before a laker-fishing trip just to fish for our bait. Gray or blue shiners seem to work almost as well, though, and buying them in bait shops is far easier and more restful than catching your own smelt.

We hook live baits on a size 10 treble hook, beneath the dorsal (back) fin. That holds it level and keeps it alive and lively. Trout get hooked easily, often even before I reach the tip-up, as they try to swallow the minnow.

I like to attach a small clip-on bobber to my tip-up line, a couple of inches below the set reel. If the flag's tripped, I can look for the bobber: If I see it, I know the wind set off the flag, a fish hit and dropped the bait, or the fish is hanging just below the hole. Bobber gone or, better yet, the reel spinning? There's a fish fight brewing. And I know where to reset the line quickly when it's over.

If it's your turn at the tip-up when the flag flies, gently take the device from the hole and peel a few more feet of line from it. Then set it in your minnow bucket so the reel won't freeze. Let the fish snug up the extra line or gently tighten it yourself, and set the hook with a slight tug. Now it's a hand-over-hand fight, one in which the fish may often demand line. Be sure to allow the rather light line to slip through your fingers before its breaking point.

The fight goes better, too, if a partner walks your tip-up away from the hole as you gain line from the fish. That reduces the chances of tangling that long piece of light line. You can call them back toward you if you need to feed more line to a running fish.

More trout are probably lost within a few feet of the hole than at any other point during the fight. Often an excited angler just doesn't react quickly enough when the fish makes another run. Some ice fishers like to use a gaff hook to haul a big fish atop the ice. I don't. I'd rather let the fish make a few more runs, and I will then start the fish's nose up the hole, grabbing it by hand behind the gill plate and pulling it atop the ice. Gaffs may be efficient, but I'd rather lose a trout than poke a hole in it. I've seen plenty of trout lost to improper or hasty gaffing, too.

A few tricks can boost your tip-up odds on lakers. One is to lift your tip-up a few feet in the air every fifteen minutes or so (holding the reel so the flag doesn't deploy and slap you in the face—personal experience). I don't know whether that jigging motion coaxes a bite from a laker that might have been thinking about gobbling the minnow, or if it just makes the bait more visible to fish in the vicinity, but I do know that many days one-half of your flags will come within minutes of jigging the tip-ups. Sometimes, too, you'll lift a tip-up to find a fish already on; it just didn't move far enough away to trip the mechanism.

I like to start my laker fishing in about 100 feet of water. Don't be afraid to move to deeper or shallower waters, though, if your first choices don't pay off. Lake trout sometimes lurk in relatively shallow water, 60 to 90 feet deep, early and late in the ice season. They generally swim deeper in midwinter, when we've caught them nearly 200 feet down in some Great Lakes bays. Whatever the depth, keep your offering near bottom; most lakers are caught from on bottom to 5 feet above it, and seldom are they found more than 10 feet above bottom. Experiment. We move any tip-up that doesn't produce after a half hour to an hour. Besides keeping boredom at bay, that expands the search for the day's hot hole. (Just remember to keep checking the safety of the ice as you move across a lake.)

Often most of a day's catch will come from one tip-up, randomly set just where some aspect of bottom contour or supply of food has them concentrated. You can sometimes even return to the same hole the next day for a fresh batch of laker action!

LAKERS ON LURES

Instead of tip-ups, some lake trout fans swear by jigging or "chugging," bobbing heavy spoons and lures on hand-lines just off bottom in the same areas in which you'd set tip-ups for lakers. Lakers (and splake) will often slam a jigging-model Rapala minnow, lead-headed jig, or heavy spoon. The Swedish Pimple is a longtime favorite among laker fishermen everywhere, and my go-to laker choice is pearl, size 7. Many lures work better if baited with a dead minnow or "sweetened" with cut bait such as flesh from a sucker.

For these bigger, baited lures, you need stout rods and heavy line to provide enough hook-setting power, and you have to make sure your hook is sharp. Low-stretch line is a plus for this deep fishing. Lake trout jiggers used Dacron line long before modern braided gel-spun lines came into fashion. Some prefer line with a lead-core within a braided sheath, or even wire line. Whatever your choice, keep it tight to impart the best action possible to the lure and, when the strike comes, set that big hook far below you.

It was once rare to see a rod and reel used for this deepwater fishing with hefty lures and stout line. Laker jiggers fashioned such fishing tools as wooden, sickle-shaped sticks with pegs for holding their line. Others used notched sticks or grooved, donut-shaped wooden devices on which their line could be wound. If using a relatively light lure such as a Jigging Rapala, Puppet Minnow, or a lighter spoon—usually in shallower waters—you can get away with a reel-equipped rod, but many of us still like the feel of the old gear.

Keep your chugging lure near bottom, where lake trout spend most of their time. Sometimes, bouncing the lure on bottom sediments seems to cause a ruckus that a greedy laker just can't pass up. I like to keep the lure moving as much as possible, changing the rhythm until finding one that produces fish. Learn to feel what your lure is doing; many times the fish will take the lure as it flutters back down after a crisp lift upwards.

A strike usually comes in one of two forms: an explosive attack that can yank your knuckles down to the ice, or a more subtle resistance that feels almost as if the trout is just gumming your lure. Either way, you'll want sharp hook points to drive home, and care must be taken as the fish is fought topside. The heavier lure can fall free if you allow any slack. But in trade, you can lean far more heavily into the fight of your fish than you could with lighter tackle.

A handmade jigging stick proved the undoing of the trout in the foreground.

Splake often behave like smaller versions of their laker parentage. (It can take a trained biologist, in a laboratory, to distinguish between the two.) In general, however, splake will be found in slightly shallower water, and occasionally farther off bottom, than lakers.

Splake will always have a hold on me, felt on my first ice-fishing outing for trout. A friend took me along one early winter day. We settled on the ice over 40 feet of water, figuring we'd fish for perch with jigging rods there while watching tip-ups set for trout at a nearby drop-off into water about 70 feet deep. We baited red teardrop lures with wax worms and lowered them on the jigging rods. My lure had barely reached bottom when it was gobbled, and the fight the 15-inch splake provided was exciting on the light rod. I was sold. The limit was then five trout per day of any species, and in a couple of hours, we'd collected our ten fish, the biggest of them weighing almost 4 pounds.

In time, we learned that 2- to 3-inch minnows were even more productive for splake than wax worms, and that the hybrid trout could be caught on either jigging rods or tip-ups.

Brown Trout on Ice

Brown trout are in many ways far different than lakers and splake, but variations on the tactics described above will also ice browns.

Unlike bottom-hugging lake trout, look for brown trout in the top 15 or 20 feet of water, whatever its depth. Browns seem more skittish than lakers, too, so downsize your tackle, and keep ice-top commotion to a minimum.

For tip-up fishing for browns, I like high-quality, clear line of 4 pounds test, 6 max. Run main lines of that weight on tip-ups rigged especially for browns, or add leaders of that line, at least 10 feet long, to heavier-rigged laker tip-ups.

Substitute a small split shot or two for the egg sinker used for lakers, only enough weight to keep the bait—blue or gray minnows 2 or 3 inches long—down. Set the tip-up as lightly as possible so the fish doesn't feel much resistance when it takes the bait. Attach a small clip-on bobber just below the set reel to make it easy to return the bait to the same depth after (hopefully) catching a brown. And set tip-ups away from the area where you'll be sitting, to keep your ice-top commotion from spooking the fish.

Reread the earlier section on fighting lake trout. The same principles apply to tip-up-caught browns, although browns can be more explosive fighters, making repeated runs. Many a belligerent brown has been lost hole-side when an impatient angler tried to ice it too soon.

Jigging works on brown trout, too, although higher in the water column.

A partner and I once stumbled onto a brown-trout bonanza. Eight-inch-thick, clear ice was rumbling, making more ice yet on this minus-10°F day, as we began lowering lures 40 feet to the bottom. We'd heard that orange, jigging-model Rapalas were good for perch here, and we caught several on the deepwater edge of a steep drop-off. But several times, a brown trout slammed the descending lure! The browns were following what we'd find to be a common winter pattern, cruising 15 to 20 feet below the ice. Sometimes they'd stop a lure as it was being lowered, sometimes they'd slam one as it was being brought topside for a weed-check. More escaped than were caught, but we iced several nice ones. Splake, some of them a foot long, were swimming among the perch, and it became a guessing game as to which fish, perch or one of the trout, would come up with the lure.

Now, we never head onto a trout lake without a few of the Rapalas, and more than once they've provided action on a slow day. A short spinning rod and reel works well for this light-action jigging, a reliable reel drag allowing you to hook and play a big fish on light line, 4 or 6 pounds test. Six-pound test will work, but if you're careful, you'll find your action improving with four-pound test. Try lighter spoons, smaller Swedish Pimples, or jigging-model Rapalas in size 5 or 7 and, especially, in bright orange.

Stationary spinning tackle can also be used for any of the trout or salmon species. Light line is favored, and the rod is propped up or set across a pail, with the bail open so a fish can take out line freely. Some tuck the line under a rubber band on the rod handle; a fish can tug it free easily. For browns or Atlantic salmon, use a clip-on bobber to keep the bait at the desired depth, and unclip it during a fish fight. Fish the bottom for lakers and splake. Leave the bait at rest, as with a tip-up, giving it a raise-and-drop jig every once in awhile. You don't have a flag to call you to action and will have to watch for line peeling off the reel. But in return you can enjoy the wild fight of a big fish on a light-action rod. A snap-trap rig is another good way to split the difference between tip-up and spinning rod fishing.

WHAT WAS IT?

A friend was fishing for brown trout with an ultra-light spinning setup on a big inland lake. Fishing 5 feet down in 10 feet of water, Tom told me, "I got two hits and caught two fish. My buddy also caught one. We thought they looked a little unusual, but we were sure they were brown trout, so we took them home and ate them."

Later, Tom got thinking again about the unusual appearance of the fish, weighing 6 pounds and 4 pounds, that he'd eaten. Browns have squared tails, and the tails of these fish were slightly forked. The spots on the sides were a little different than those on most brown trout, too, and the fish turned blue-gray as they lay on the ice, instead of assuming the darker tones normally seen in iced brown trout.

A couple of his friends suggested that maybe the fish were Atlantic salmon. That thought had crossed Tom's mind, too, but he hadn't heard of any stocking of those fish, close cousins to brown trout and often difficult to distinguish from them.

"Then," Tom said, "I found out that the Department of Natural Resources had planted 1,600 Atlantics in that lake two years earlier, and that they would have been about the size of the ones we caught. I could have kicked myself. I wanted a nice Atlantic salmon to [have mounted and] put on the wall."

Grumbling but determined, Tom returned to the lake a few days later. Sure enough, he caught another Atlantic salmon, this one a 4½-pounder, and sped it to a taxidermist.

SMALL TROUT, BIG THRILLS

In some lakes brook trout are legal year-round, and fishing for them in winter is a delicate, thrilling pursuit.

I remember lying on my belly on a small inland lake, watching a grub-baited teardrop on 4-pound test line as it bobbed 3 feet down in clear waters 4 feet deep.

Occasionally the snout of a bright-colored brookie poked out, and the trout, with a sudden burst of speed, would attack the bait. Sometimes I'd be quick enough setting the hook and flipped the trout onto the snowy ice, but more often the fish would hit and run, sometimes escaping with my bait, while I was left lying in the snow, a smile pasted on my face, maybe even chuckling aloud.

The closest comparison I can think of is teasing a cat with a feather on a string. It's worth the effort to find lakes open for winter brookie fishing.

OVER THE RAINBOW

Rainbow trout opportunities are more widespread. Many lakes, large and small, offer planted populations of 'bows, and they'll fall for a variety of ice-fishing methods.

Panfish-style but with rods and reels ready for a savage strike and fierce fight, fish within 6 feet of bottom, using a limber rod lined with monofilament of 2 or 4 pounds test. Good lures include teardrops, small jigs, ice flies, and small spoons. Bait them with wax worms, corn borers, wigglers, small minnows, crayfish, or salmon eggs. Corn is a longtime favorite of rainbow anglers, too.

If your state allows it, "chumming," dispersing underwater corn, salmon eggs, or even oatmeal, often draws in fish and boosts the action. The trout quickly find this source of food, and the nearby lure you're offering.

Many ice anglers find night-fishing best for rainbows, especially when using artificial light and chum as described above. In shallow water or on clear ice, a lantern near your fishing hole may draw fish closer. Some anglers even use 12-volt lights, protected from the water in a sealed glass jar, or a commercially made underwater fishing light, lowered to fish level to attract trout. (The same trick often works on crappies!)

Where?

Most winter trout (and salmon) lakes offer fish planted by conservation departments. Usually released at fingerling length, browns and rainbows may begin showing up in the catch just a year or two later, while lakers take longer to mature—at least three years old before they really start showing up in angler harvests, and then only in the 14- to 18-inch range. (Some really big lakers from cold, clear water—the trophy 20-pounders that make news everywhere—may be twenty years old.)

Begin your trout-lake research by checking with local fish biologists or your fisheries department's web page, to learn which lakes have been planted with trout and when.

And when winter moves in and drives late-season boat anglers off your favorite trout lake, big or small, home to any trout species, wait only until the ice is good and safe—and then head onto it!

CHAPTER 18

Laker Country

RAINBOW TROUT FROM THE PACIFIC NORTHWEST ARE NOW RESIDENT in dozens of states. Atlantic salmon swim in Midwest waters and beyond. Brown trout came here from Germany. We've planted Pacific Ocean coho and chinook salmon in the Great Lakes and other inland waters. We've swapped bass, walleyes, and trout from lake to lake. We've even built striper–white bass hybrids, pike-muskie crosses, and lake trout–brook trout crosses and backcrosses.

Many of those newcomers offer great attributes. Browns and rainbows, including their "steelhead" clan, are considered locals. Ditto the cool-water species described above. The "wiper" fights well; the splake is easily caught and a tasty delight. The tiger musky grows quickly to provide top-flight fishing action.

The true native lake trout, meanwhile, roams at the bottom of its native lakes. Known regionally as the laker, togue, mackinaw, or gray trout, it feeds pragmatically upon whatever living or dead matter it finds. It may take four growing seasons or more for that prowling to produce an 18-inch fish. Not famously fierce in battle nor described as stunning on the table, it performs credibly in both areas. Much of the laker's magic, though, comes from the places where you find it.

The mackinaw thrives only where lakes are deep, clear, and cold. Those regions are home also to whitefish, ciscoes, and others, but the laker reigns, the top consumer in the food chain. It's a dark, cold-water

Battle nearly over, an angler eases a lake trout onto the ice.

world 100 feet or more below the surface, down where water temperatures are in the low 50s. Togue thrive there; you'd be hypothermic in minutes.

Laker angling is as unusual as the quarry itself. As an angler, you generally don't get close to a lake trout until you've fooled him. Most fishing is based at least 70 feet above the trout, often double that amount or more. That's a long line of faith running from your fishing rig to the lure or bait.

Since typical laker lures dance and weave wildly below the ice, gray-trout fishermen can't sit shoulder-to-shoulder as can perch or panfish fans; lure-holding lines would quickly become tangled. So lake-trout fishing is a relatively solitary pursuit—a heavily clad angler perhaps a few dozen yards from their angling partner and likely a few hundred yards from fishing neighbors outside the party.

That's the barren social setting, and few of us would have it any other way. For all the fanciness we build into our equipment and strategies, we still like simple fishing and sometimes just our own company.

As a general rule, you either offer the laker a live or dead bait suspended on a tip-up or other stationary fishing device, or you bob a lure, baited or unbaited, and hope to attract the fish's interest. Either approach is limited to the last few feet before bottom, and you might expect to pass an hour or several between bites.

Laker anglers are a little different from other anglers. They're not quite as action-oriented as panfish anglers or pike fans. They are—and must be—a little more willing to watch smoke curl smoothly from the chimney of a barely visible cabin on a far-off shore, tracing the path of that smoke as it snakes through the pines and onto the lake.

Most gray-trout fans who bob lures can't even tell you what action they gave the lure just before a strike came; they were hypnotized by the cadence and the setting, and the strike surprised them, maybe more than the hook surprised the trout.

Laker devotees love to watch an entire shoreline disappear in a snowstorm. Sometimes, a mile or two out on a big, deepwater lake, the quality of light changes. Dark colors get darker, more intense, while light shades grow lighter, clearer. About the time the scene has nearly faded to black and white, the snow arrives.

The first few flakes zip by quickly. Check your coat sleeve to make sure it was snow. Ask your partner if they've seen it, too. The cloud slowly moving offshore at lake level appears half-haze, half-precipitation, and you quickly double-check the compass heading back to the car. You've been here before. In a few minutes the red cabin to the south, that small one behind the tall pine, starts to fade from sight. There, the stored snow just blew out of the big tree, adding fuel to the mini-blizzard moving toward you and your tip-ups. The other cabins along the lake are now beginning to fade away, too. They don't just disappear—they wash out. The snow in the mile in between gradually builds in intensity and the picture becomes less distinct, finally disappearing.

You may be a little uncomfortable at first when only the magnetic needle of the compass links you to your car, its heater, and, eventually, home, but there's not much you can do about it now. And once the shore's gone, a certain home-in-the-wild feeling arrives.

Suddenly it's not so cold, and you're somehow more confident in your ability to handle what nature throws your way. You grab the skimmer and ladle slush from the fishing holes. You gather the scattered gear so it won't get snow-buried and lost. And you settle back down to watch both your tip-ups and the ghost of the shoreline.

Even in the heaviest of snows, the shoreline will usually fade back into view from time to time. And eventually, the snows will slacken and the cabins pop back out of the cloud.

If that happens before you've finished fishing, you'll be almost sorry that it has.

If you don't like watching the cabins fade away, I'm betting that you won't much like lake-trout fishing. For the laker is prized as much for what it is and where it lives as for what it does. It's a rather solitary fish in a rather harsh environment.

So, too, is the lake-trout angler, albeit only for a precious few hours each winter.

CHAPTER 19

Etcetera Species

THE FISH SPECIES ON WHICH WE'VE FOCUSED IN OTHER CHAPTERS ARE widely available. Here are three that are a bit novel—but plenty of fun to meet, catch, and eat!

WHITEFISH

Lake or "common" whitefish and lake trout are natural winter neighbors, haunting the same deep waters. Take another look at the tips we provided for jigging for lake trout in the trout-fishing chapter; we'll be adjusting them only slightly for whitefish fishing.

Most whitefish anglers use traditional methods, chugging hefty Swedish Pimples or other heavy lures on low-stretch braided line; Dacron was the original material used, and many still use it. Others opt for newer braids. The line is simply wound around a stick, which is then used as a primitive jigging rod. I have one friend who, despite lots of more refined tackle, still believes the rough chugging stick does the best job. "I think I catch more fish with a stick," he says. "I have a little more control over the lure and can give it just the action I want. I can twitch it and barely move it. I just get a better feel of what's going on down there." (Of course, part of the reason he catches more fish on the stick is he does much of his fishing with it!)

And the braided line, with its reduced stretch compared to monofilament, makes it far easier to set the hook in a fish as far as 150 feet below you. A good combination is 18-pound test Dacron, with a 6-foot leader

A whitefish can be a tasty prize for an ice angler.

of 12- to 17-pound test monofilament or fluorocarbon line running to the lure.

If building your own stick, craft it to a known length so you can count line wraps to determine the depth you're fishing. That's especially helpful if you're not using an electronic flasher or sounder. That way, you can duplicate your presentation if it proves successful. Most whitefish fisheries begin in relatively shallow water when ice first forms, moving deeper as winter deepens and shallower again as spring approaches. Yesterday's success is your best clue for today's fishing.

An option to the chugging stick is a short spinning rod, equipped with an open-face spinning reel loaded with 8- or 10-pound test monofilament. Setting the hook with the spinning outfit is a little more challenging because of the bend of the rod and stretch of the line, but it's far easier to keep the line tight. That's a roughly even trade-off; reeling in line neatly instead of laying a hopeless tangle of braided line on the ice is really appreciated in cold, blustery weather.

Whitefish techniques are really quite simple. White Swedish Pimples in size 7 are most popular, sometimes dressed up with a green or red dot or a colored or silver "flicker" on the lower split ring. Some whitefish experts add a barrel swivel between the hook and lure, to extend the reach of the hook a little. Others add another treble hook to the split ring at the top of the lure. I've brought several whitefish onto the ice, the top hook securely in their mouths and the factory-installed hooks dangling free.

Some days the whitefish really seem to respond to the addition of skeined eggs from trout, salmon, whitefish, or perch. Tied spawn bags don't seem quite as successful.

A soft jigging action of a foot or so seems most effective; use milder strokes than you would for lake trout. (And don't be surprised if your catch mixes lake trout and whitefish, since they favor the same areas.)

Whitefish, while not strictly a schooling fish, often congregate around food sources. Start in about 90 feet of water, and try chugging the lure fifty or seventy-five times. If there's no action, move, and keep moving deeper until you either find fish or give up. You can, if it's legal where you fish, cultivate your own fishing hot spot by chumming with corn, fish eggs, or even fish scales.

My whitefish-fan friend offers a tip: "If one guy is in the same spot for very long, I become suspicious. If I'm in a wandering mood and not catching fish, I go over," closer but not uncomfortably close.

BURBOT

If you fish for lake trout long enough in one of the big, deep lakes in which they're native, sooner or later you're likely to catch a burbot.

You might be introduced to it by another name—eelpout, ling, lawyer, cusk, ling cod—the last a reference to its membership in the saltwater cod family, which it resembles in fine flavor. Whatever the name by which you know it, I guarantee you won't forget your first one.

The body is long and relatively slender, at least once past the rib structures. The head is large, relatively flat, and features one chin barbell or whisker. It has two dorsal fins, one running back almost to the tail. It is greenish-black and, when brought up from the depths at which it normally swims, the eel-like body often coils from the change in pressure. Before you can enjoy its superb taste, you have to get past its appearance—unusual at best, perhaps even ugly.

Most burbot are caught incidentally by anglers trying for lake trout or, less frequently, walleyes. In daylight ling cod generally haunt waters frequented by lakers, 80 to 200 feet deep. But lawyers have been found in depths of 700 feet, and as shallow as 1 to 4 feet at late-winter spawning time.

Biologists say burbot feed mainly at night, often in waters just 15 to 20 feet deep, although we've found these greedy feeders will often set a deepwater tip-up flag flying at midday. They like fish, crayfish, and other organic foods, and will readily chomp on the minnows or smelt, alive or dead, you offer lake trout. Once hooked they wage an impressive battle, at least as gamely as a lake trout.

Burbot offer plenty of resistance when they're at bottom, and sometimes the fish just can't be budged by the angler above. As the fish is brought topside, however, the change in pressure removes some of the zip, and odds quickly turn in the angler's favor.

And despite their off-putting appearance, some anglers prize them for the table. The flesh is firm, white, and very mild-flavored, low in oil

A young angler considers an unusual catch—a burbot.

and relatively free of bones. Their large livers, which some call very tasty, are high in vitamins A and D.

Burbot are caught on Great Lakes bays and from many larger, cold-water inland lakes across the North American ice belt. The fish is interesting, as are the reactions of the anglers who catch one. Among other oddities, they're said to wrap their tails around an arm of their captor. Some anglers kill burbot and leave them on the ice for the seagulls, but others call them "gentlemen's catfish" and happily collect them for the dinner table. Special tackle and seasonal regulations often apply to them, and some communities even celebrate them in fun festivals.

"I'd almost as soon have a lawyer as a trout," one regular lake-trout angler told me one day, as he iced his fourth burbot of the day.

A fisheries biologist told me, "Burbot are a tremendous fish. They have an awfully large liver, and the liver is a real delicacy, probably the best part of the fish." He said the liver can be cooked by rolling it in a batter and deep-fat-frying it, just like other fish.

The long tail is flanked with clean, white meat. Cut into narrow strips and boiled in salted water, this "freshwater lobster," as its nickname suggests, tastes like lobster or other seafood. Frying the fillets is also popular.

The best way to catch a burbot, I think, is to go after lake trout. But while lakers can often be found anywhere in the first 10 feet of water off bottom, the burbot is almost always right on bottom.

SMELT

What is the smallest fish to consistently draw the interest of ice anglers? I'm betting it's the smelt, which has plenty of fans for two very good reasons: The smelt is one of the deadliest baits for lake trout, splake, and northern pike fishing. And fried smelt, especially those caught in winter, are a tasty delight.

(One drawback: Like other fish species, smelt from some Great Lakes waters have joined the list of species for which human consumption advisories have been issued; check with your state fisheries or health department for details.)

Where I live, spring was long thought to arrive only when large schools of smelt would gather at certain Great Lakes shorelines to stage

Bait or bite? A smelt poses the question.

spring spawning runs, met there by wader-clad anglers with hand nets, intent on filling buckets with smelt.

You're not apt to collect catches of that magnitude through the ice, but winter smelt seem firmer, with better-tasting meat. That's if you plan to eat them; if you have a big-game fishing trip coming, the best bait in the world is in your bucket. Many pike and lake-trout anglers agree that a live smelt will often out-catch other bait they can offer. A dead smelt is a close second.

Fish for your bait? My dad would always laugh when telling others how his son and friends would drive an hour to a deep lake to fish half the night for smelt—just to drive to another deep, far-off lake long before daylight the next day with a fresh supply of bait for lake-trout fishing. But he knew that boosted our odds of dropping off a laker fillet later.

Most smelt fishing takes place at night, sometimes from shanties equipped with large reels that allow a fish to be iced quickly and the bait re-lowered. More often today, anglers use light spinning rigs whose reliable reels make catching smelt and returning the lure and bait to productive waters a breeze.

The portable angler can find good success fishing in the open at night. Drill your fishing holes and pile up the resulting slush in the center of the pattern of holes, usually four holes about 6 feet apart for two anglers. The slush will provide a platform for your gasoline or propane lantern, which will both illuminate your fishing and sometimes attract smelt beneath the ice. Three- or four-pound test monofilament line works well. Many smelt anglers bait small hooks or teardrop-shaped lures with small, "pinhead" minnows, but I've had good luck with wax worms or other grubs, and they're a lot easier to handle. Until smelt reach lengths of 5 or 6 inches, biologists say, their diet consists mainly of small plants and animals, crustaceans, worms, and insects. After that they begin to rely more on fish.

Get your group to spread out offerings vertically to fish various depths and discover where smelt are swimming that night—anywhere from just under the ice to near bottom in 40 feet of water or more.

Get your smelt atop the ice quickly if you'll be using them for bait, and unhook and drop them into a cooler filled with water from the lake in which you're fishing. At home, an aquarium-type or bait-bucket aerator helps keep them alive. If some die, keep them frozen solid in a freezer for another fishing trip. Dead smelt often out-catch live minnows.

None of those concerns are real if you're planning to cook up a midwinter mess of smelt. Once you do, you may not go back to store-bought or spring-caught smelt.

Be sure to save a few lively ones for bait, though.

CHAPTER 20

Specifics, Not Species

ACROSS WHAT SEEMS LIKE AN ICE AGE, I'VE SHARED BUCKETS AND benches, shelters, and open lake tops with myriad anglers, and learned lots from each of them. But a few pros have stood out, fast and easily becoming friends, companions, and mentors.

I wish you such good fortune.

These guys—they happen to be males but needn't be—I've seen every few years, not every week, and in places from summertime tackle shows to ice-bound lakes. Invariably I return with a notebook filled with specific tactics for certain fish species, and around them I've built newspaper and magazine articles, and even book chapters. But there are almost always stray tips that cut across species lines—principles of ice fishing that apply whether you're after walleye or pike, bluegills or brown trout.

That general expertise—plus some non-species-specific stuff I've picked up on my own—is what this chapter's all about.

It's not everything they teach, and they might have even moved on from some ideas, but these suggestions have changed my ice fishing for the better.

Pull up a pail. Here are some ideas that might boost your catch and increase your fun.

DAVE GENZ, who launched the modernization of ice fishing, has the uncanny ability to look at an ice-fishing puzzle and find a novel solution.

Fish Trap flip-over shelter. Genz Pack mount for a truly ice-portable Vexilar sounder. Suits made of shelter material. Rods and reels perfect

Ice-fishing pioneer Dave Genz demonstrates the stovepipe-style fishing and lure testing unit he built into his open-water boat—to simulate ice fishing!

matches for lures that show up splendidly on electronics. And then there's his "Hole-E Boat."

In that flat-bottom boat, an 8-inch-diameter pipe rises from the floor so Genz can drop a line and lure into it, monitoring on Vexilar flashers mounted nearby the structure, fish, and lure. This fun and productive twist on summer fishing is also a great way to test ice lures, and the better you know exactly how your lure acts underwater, the better you can manipulate it. I haven't cut a hole in the bottom of my boat, but I have been reminded to study how one lure acts underwater before rushing out to buy new, equally untested ones.

Seek balance, Genz advises. It sounds like Zen, but it's just good ice-fishing strategy. Long ago he surprised me when he said he didn't pay a lot of attention to line diameter or thickness—that is, its makeup or strength. A bigger priority, he said, was that rod, lure, and line balance. "What matters is that the lure can stretch the line tight so you can tell what's going on." He assembles his fishing rigs by line weight, not by species. "I don't have a bluegill rig and a walleye rig. I have a 2-pound rig and an 8-pound rig."

Adjust your lure on the line so it sits level, he said, particularly jigs that hang horizontally. Catch a fish, or even strike but miss a fish, and the eye of the lure can slide within the knot so that it hangs oddly. A hot bite can turn cold when the presentation's unnatural.

Lure color? Not a big issue to Genz. "First [priority] is depth. Then lure speed. Then maybe color." OK, among favorite colors he lists orange and chartreuse, green and chartreuse, and glow.

Pinch the barb(s) on a lure to make it easier to put on bait, which Genz preaches you should do often—after every fish at least. "People change minnows often, but with a worm they tend to rethread it on. It only takes a second to rebait, and now you're going to catch another fish." Slow-moving winter fish have plenty of time to examine an offering, and a fresh, fat one will draw more takers.

Speed things up, Genz advises. "Pick up the pace" of your lure jigging, Genz says. "Move it away a little bit, get him to chase it, and pretty soon you'll catch that fish. Bang it on the bottom, keep that cadence going while bringing it up slowly. If I do all that and still nothing—I'm out of there," off to try new spots or at least new fish.

Follow the sun. Genz fishes all day but tracks the approach of the evening's "golden hour, when the sun hits the trees." Fish often become more active then; as the shadows lengthen, he makes sure he's in his best locations for that hour.

GO TO SCHOOL. Mark Martin of Twin Lake, Michigan, has a well-established and well-attended Ice Fishing Vacation School, in which ice anglers "camp" in a lakeside hotel and combine classroom and on-ice time under his tutelage and that of his carefully selected instructors. That's a great way to learn more about the sport.

Others? Watch for workshops put on by state natural resource agencies, pro appearances at sporting goods stores, and clinics offered at sport shows. Pick up a trick or two at each stop, and soon you'll be the expert!

From my attendance at sessions of Martin's school:

"**Safety** is the number-one thing," said Martin, after shortening a fishing day when gale-force-plus winds were forecast. "I used to have no fear, but the more time you put in on the ice, you start seeing [why safety is important]. Creepers, [self-rescue] spikes. Stick by the rules—always come back off the ice."

Don't check your bait too soon after missing a bite. Instead of reeling up, Martin said, drop the lure to the bottom, bang it there a few times to stir up sediments, and then lift it a bit and wait. Often, a strike results.

Snaps make changing out jigging lures easier, and make you more likely to actually do it.

A barrel swivel between the main line and leader reduces line twist.

Mix methods. With two people in a shanty, have one jig and the other tend a "dead stick," an unmoved line and lure. Fish seem drawn by the jigged lure but willing to close the deal on the unmoved one. "Two jigging [next to each other]," said Martin, "just doesn't get it."

Set tip-ups close. "It's like having more dead-stick rods," said Martin. Fish drawn by jigging might bite minnows. "If they come in for a jig, see something twisting in the current, it's too much for them to resist."

BRIAN "BRO" BROSDAHL, super-angler, guide, fishing educator, and good-natured showman, may just be the world's biggest ice-fishing kid. He exudes enthusiasm and is always willing to try something new and share it if it works.

That probably stems from his youth, when an early memory features an ice-caught crappie—and his father urging him not to keep every big fish he caught.

Good thing. He's caught a lot of them.

Bloodworm basics. Bro has made a specialty of studying the little critters on the lake bottom that play key roles in the diets of fish and offerings of successful anglers. In fact, that's the biggest impact Bro's had on me, getting me to think about the food web arising from the lake bottom, instead of sprinkling down like the lures and baits we offer. The lures he's helped design have buggy eyes, hatching-critter profiles, and other features that fool fish into thinking their next meal just arrived—from the bottom.

Brosdahl first turned many of us on to bloodworms, critters that hatch into midge flies in summer. "They're at the base of the food chain. Without bloodworms, our fishing would end. They feed on decaying matter, and they feed minnows and gamefish. Every square foot of the lake bottom that's fertile is just full of them—weed beds, mud, hard bottom. When weeds die, bloodworms eat them. They're great little garbage feeders."

Brosdahl said bloodworms generally remain in the soft bottom of a lake during the day, "and at night they wriggle out of their holes. They really come out."

Because of the way a fish-finder works, the bottom-haunting worms aren't visible on the screen. Nor are the lures and baits you send down there to imitate them.

But fish see and gobble those lures and baits, especially buggy-looking lures (his own Bro Bug, from Northland Tackle, an industry leader) baited with plastic imitations.

Bro still fishes with live bait, but more and more he reaches for plastic bloodworm imitations. "You get action out of plastic you just can't get out of live bait."

Go glow: Anglers have long used lures painted with phosphorescent paint that they charged with a light source. Now, replaceable, exposed glow sticks in lures do the job, and do it well. Bro said the Northland Glo-Shot Spoon, armed with a glow light stick, has become his first lure down the hole most of the time, because it draws the most active and often biggest fish. He even uses it in a dead-stick presentation, where the glowing color adds allure.

Heavy metal: Brosdahl is big on lures made of tungsten, a relatively new and still-evolving category. Thirty percent heavier than lead, "tungsten is a really awesome metal for fishing," said Brosdahl.

He described tungsten lures as "not so much heavier but small for their weight," before admitting with a chuckle those were different ways of saying the same thing. Smaller lure at the same weight, or heavier lure at the same size.

Tungsten keeps line tight with smaller lures. It helps you "pound" the bottom to stir up sediment and fishy interest. Lures plummet to get back to active schools of fish.

That all matters most in deep water, said Brosdahl. "Shallow, go ahead and use lead," he advised.

Tungsten lures, from several manufacturers, cost more than lead and are a bit more delicate, especially at hook-removal time. New tools help with that.

They also get the nod on waters where lead-based tackle isn't allowed.

WHAT'S MY LINE? Many newer ice-fishing lines are special formulations of monofilament nylon and fluorocarbon, cofilament, or braided lines of several materials and constructions. They're all good, and very good for specific applications.

But pike anglers caught northerns on tip-ups wrapped with simple, black braided line for decades, and still can and still do. Panfishers once used more 4-pound test monofilament line, Stren or Trilene or their equivalent, than anything else, and iced plenty of bluegills and crappies. Bump that mono up to 6 or 8 pounds test, and you're ready for perch, walleyes, or trout.

THE "HOLE" TRUTH: I've been a mainly foot-powered ice angler for decades, and a big job on most outings was lugging the right tool for creating a hole in the ice.

Modern electric augers such as the StrikeMaster Lithium 24v
are lightweight, all-day hole-boring wonders.

Time was, you couldn't do much better than a cup-shaped hand auger. It edged out the spud, the long-handled chisel, when it came time to make a hole in ice a foot thick or thicker. But it was slow going, and keeping or returning a sharp edge to the cup was a task many of us never seemed to master.

Just in time, the Swedish two-blade auger arrived, led by StrikeMaster. In its original blue form, or its incredibly improved Lazer hand auger, this hand drill swiftly and cleanly spun holes from a few to a whopping

8 inches across. You could (carefully) sharpen the blades, or ship them to a shop for sharpening, or replace them with blades hanging on a hook in nearly every bait shop in ice country.

Meanwhile, gas engines roared onto the ice. They were great—unless you carried in your genes an internal combustion curse like mine, or were on foot like my pals and me, lugging equipment sleds or shelters behind us. Every pound counts, then, and for most trips the weight of a gas drill was just too much. A friend carried his gas auger over his shoulder, to lighten the sled's load.

Up rose electric drills, including StrikeMaster's pioneering Electra Lazer, powered by a 12-volt gel battery like those on sounders. I bought the first one I saw and loved the way it grumbled through thick ice. It was, though, a bit heavy, and on many days the battery ran out of juice well before we ran out of interest.

Refinements came in gas-powered augers—including one I owned briefly that had so much torque I visited my physical therapist as often as my favorite lake.

Don't forget: Fishing began as a food-gathering pursuit. A fine day can close with a great fish fry!

Now comes the StrikeMaster Lithium 24v Auger, the tough little brother to the Lithium 40v and Pro Lithium 40v Lite. It seems to have found the sweet spot between mechanized hole-cutting and non-mechanized ice travel.

The 40-volt powerhouses will punch 100 to 115 holes through 16 inches of ice, but the Lithium 24 will bore 50 holes, and there just aren't that many days when a party of three or four anglers want to drill more than that. Several times we've planned to drill and count holes until the battery ran out—but we ran out of energy before the Lithium 24v did. (A spare battery would provide backup if needed.) It's light in the sled, and its torque is forgiving to mature shoulders.

Drilling holes next to anglers using cordless drill units—another extremely popular format, especially among those who already own construction-grade drills—we've appreciated the fact that the Power Point keeps the drill in place while spinning; our neighbors sometimes had to dance out of the way of an errant drill. But fair is fair: Others flat-out love their electric drills, be they dedicated or drill-powered. Gas, though, does seem on the way out.

OLDE LANG SYNE. "It is amazing how many ice fishermen are still fishing with their grandfather's equipment and are proud of it," said Dave Genz after helping to fill a pail with foot-long perch. "It's good to be proud of the old equipment—but not so good to fish with it."

Once in awhile, though, I think it's good to fish with the old stuff.

Pulling the vintage sled, setting simpler tip-ups, even struggling with an obsolete hand auger—they all connect you with angling and anglers

Sometimes it's fun and illuminating to ice-fish with vintage gear.

A fine fish, a muskellunge, released to fight again.

from your past, and increase your appreciation for the great gear we have available today.

And so I try each year to at least once cut a spearing hole with a hundred-year-old ice saw bought on eBay, or rig a tip-up as old as I am from a metal film-canister selection of hooks, swivels, and sinkers. I'll jig with a wooden stick.

It's connection. Celebration. Appreciation.

BE A BELIEVER. If there's one common trait of every truly expert ice angler I've ever met, it's their self-confidence, their absolute belief in their approach, methods, and tackle. They know they're going to catch a fish on the next try. Even if their belief conflicts with that of the expert next to them!

CONSERVATION ADVICE?

Eat some.

Release some.

Repeat often!

CHAPTER 21

Ice Angler's Sunset

A FROZEN LAKE KNOWS WHEN SUNDOWN IS COMING. SEVERAL HOURS before dark, its ice begins to retighten, rumbling thunderously as changing temperatures shift it about. Anglers stir, too, as the sun that shone so brightly all afternoon now dips in the southwest, and chilling breezes blow across the frozen expanse.

What a day it has been. "Wonder what the rich folks did today?" one buddy muses aloud, as he kicks warmth back into slightly numbed toes. "If they're smart, they're out here somewhere," another responds, pointing across the big frozen lake. Everything's just right. The walk back to the car or cabin is just long enough to build up a warming head of steam. We don't have buckets filled with minnows to lug along. The fish we've caught far outweigh those early-morning minnows, but somehow they're less a load.

We've watched an entire day unfold on this winter lake, each section of that day a separate memory. Together they form a master's quilt of pleasure.

This morning we stood at the edge of the lake, pulling on heavy clothes and yelling at one adventurer to close the van door while we did. We gathered more gear than we could ever need, each of us still forgetting at least one piece of equipment we really could use. Buckets and boxes filled with tip-ups, jig rods, lures, and terminal tackle. A bag of cheese and nuts in one of them, a vacuum bottle of coffee in another. I stashed a camera in a fanny pack and carried a minnow bucket in hand. You pulled a sled laden with a power auger.

Your kid, just twelve years old, grabbed whatever was left and self-consciously made sure he lugged his fair share.

Onto the lake, then. Walking, as it always seems in winter, into the wind. The crispness takes your breath away in a minute, and oft-clogged winter noses quickly loosen. You can sometimes tell what kind of day it's going to be by the way your face feels on the way out.

If your cheeks smart just a little, it's from dry cold. The air is clear, so there's little chance of snow or, worse yet, rain. We were halfway to the area we wanted to fish and no breath had frozen on my mustache. That meant it was relatively warm, or the air relatively moisture-free. (I remember the trout-fishing day my breath froze into solid ice, welding mustache to beard so firmly that, three hours into the fishing, I couldn't get my mouth open wide enough to eat a sandwich. We found out later it was 30°F below zero.)

If there's wetness in the air, there are two possibilities. One is that snow is coming. Maybe by noon it will be difficult to spot our farthest tip-ups. And chances are we'd then pack up early enough to get home before dark, even on slippery roads. Maybe it will be warm and damp, that combination that lets you leave your gloves off but keeps you from kneeling in the sloppy snow.

The sun peeping over the horizon gives more weather clues. Today it was clear and bright, along with the sky around it. I bet then, based upon past experience, that our best action would come from daybreak to 9 a.m. and from 3 p.m. to dark.

Again, I bet wrong.

It was almost noon when Chuck, that twelve-year-old of yours, spied the tip-up flag being released even before it was freely flying. He was off his bucket seat even before we knew anything was afoot. He was ready to fight a trout.

The trout was ready for a fight, too, spinning the reel madly as it made for water even deeper than the 100 feet in which the bait was hung. Like a pro Chuck lifted the tip-up carefully from the hole, setting it in the minnow bucket he'd grabbed on his way. (He's a clear thinker; most of the time we forget to grab the bucket and have to send someone back for it.) Putting the reel underwater keeps it from freezing during the fight and makes re-rigging far easier.

As he set the tip-up aside, Chuck deftly spun a few more yards of line off the reel, leaving some slack between him and the fish. When the fish took up that slack, Chuck yanked the hook home and began the fight.

I snapped pictures as you and Chuck bent over the hole, you giving him a few pointers on snaking in monofilament line hand-over-hand, and he tolerant enough to accept those tips. When the fish finally came into view, he silently eased it closer to the hole in the ice while you dropped your gloves in the snow and rolled up your sleeves. The fish tired and Chuck started the big lake trout's head up through the hole. You grabbed it around its body, behind the head, and with one quick move the 7-pounder flopped onto the ice, staining the snow with a few drops of crimson blood splash of sadness on a field of cheery white.

Quietly Chuck pulled the hook out of his first big trout, then carried the fish 20 feet away from the hole, to where it couldn't possibly flop its way back to freedom. You and I both silently watched him as he laid the dying fish in the snow, gently wiping away the blood and slush from its green and gray body.

You and I have caught a lot of fish from a lot of winter lakes. We've caught them fishing as a two-angler team. We've caught them in parties of a half dozen anglers. Some of our partners will fish with us no more, taken from us between ice seasons. Others have simply drifted off to different sports, different spots, or different friends.

I can't think of a fish I enjoyed more than the one Chuck caught today—a fish in whose capture I really had no part. I was flattered when Chuck used some of the tricks we taught him, impressed with the classy touches he provided himself. And uplifted with the reverence he showed the fish—proud to have taken it, with none of that adolescent thrill-of-the-kill that's exhibited by too damned many anglers of all ages.

It's kind of sad, maybe, to think that this youngster has passed the stage when ice fishing meant running across a frozen lake, sliding in the snow like a baserunner stealing third. Now he's one of the team. He'll stand back the next time a tip-up flag flies and there's another newcomer with us; he'll let the new guy take the first fish. God, he might even start drilling the holes for us, his angling companions getting (in his eyes) so advanced in years. When we're gone he might even tell the kind of stories on us that we've told him about others.

Yes, this is an especially sweet sundown, even though we're buzzing down the highway as the orb finally dips below the horizon. We'll let Chuck watch for deer along the two-lane this time; it's a good incentive for him to keep eyes open instead of dozing in the back of the van.

The miles tick off, the radio plays softly. There's little talking among our trio of anglers, probably for at least a couple of reasons.

One, there's little left to be said. Well before daylight this morning, along this same highway, we chatted incessantly, hatching plots against the well-being of every fish in the big lake. Minnows and breakfasts and tackle all blended into the verbal collage. But that was before those theories had been tested, those minnows offered, and the food burned up in cold-weather activity. Now we've had cold air fuel-injected into our lungs, eyes, and souls, and the return to warmth has brought on a heavy dose of drowsiness. Thanks again for staying awake while I drive.

(Chuck's sitting on the van's bed. I just saw him lean over the five-gallon pail to brush snow off that trout of his one more time.)

Home, we'll spread our fish out on newspapers and fillet them, taking care not to let sleepiness leave us sliced by a knife. Tomorrow, I'm going to fry up a couple of chunks and freeze the rest. Or maybe not. Fresh fish is best, so I'll drop off some to friends and relatives who listen to our ice-talk all year.

The pattern's the same, after all, year after year. About July, when the temperatures first poke into those unbearable 90s, we wait for the next batch of cool weather. When it arrives we burst in on unsuspecting golfers, water-skiers, or picnickers, advising them that it's "making ice!" Those around us shake their heads, diving back into a swimming pool or watermelon.

They don't understand, after all, that ice fishing is a year-round state of mind. Weeks after midsummer's longest day, the lake hits its seasonal temperature peak. Past that high point it's in the process of making ice, even if that solid water doesn't take shape for five months.

I know your car has perch-fishing spoons in the glove compartment all year. There's a battered jigging rod ever-ready on my desk.

Maybe, though, we are a little crazy. I'm talking to myself silently, you're watching the woods along the road, and Chuck's examining his fish again.

Here's the ski slope next to the highway. We each crane our necks to see how many neon-clad Alpiners are afoot there. The parking lot's full again. The skiers are kindred souls, since they're outdoor- and winter-minded. And I'm selfishly glad they're clustered on these constructed hills instead of on our favorite lake. But it would be neat to see how they'd react to a day of our sport.

The outdoors is never so magical as on a frozen lake where smoke from a woodstove is more visible than the cabin from which it issues. Where you test a dozen clues and theories assembled on past trips. Where neither partner in a fish-landed handshake can feel the hand of the other through thick gloves.

It's a magical world that ice anglers share on every frozen lake, and there's room for more.

Ice fishing creates many a winter memory—and yearning for the next outing.

Plenty of room, that is, if they've got their minds right.

Remember the handbill we found plastered on our windshield along the frozen warmwater lake just a few miles from home?

We'd parked the car on the road and walked down the hill for years, vaguely aware that it was legally an access site only for residents of the subdivision, not everyone. These folks had been nice and allowed literally hundreds of anglers to slide down the steep bank onto the lake, year after year.

"Dear Fishermen," the handbill began, in male-dominated language that seems off-key today but wasn't then. "The folks who live in this subdivision would like your help.

"We believe that people should enjoy the lake and we like to see people having a good time.

"We have, however, a problem that a FEW people are causing us. Most of the fishermen try to be considerate and cooperative with the property owners of the subdivision.

"The heavy snows have created even more of a parking problem. If cars are parked at the corner of the drive and the lane, other cars have difficulty getting around the corner. The school bus has had to back out and onto the road because the driver could not get the bus around the corner.

"We ask that you not park near the mailboxes, block the driveways, or park across from a driveway. Please try to park on just one side of the roadway.

"The access at the corner is not a public access. This access is owned by the residents on the west side of the road so that they have a right-of-way to the lake.

"People who are not residents of the subdivision have been permitted to reach the lake through the access. We hope we can continue this.

"Some believe the subdivision to be their personal dumping grounds for bottles, cans, trash, papers, and ashtrays. Look at the litter left on the lake. Those bottles and cans are going to float into swimming areas this summer, causing more cut feet on children.

"A few have found it clever to use obscenities toward the women and children on the street.

"Remember the guy that found it necessary to spud three holes in the middle of a small area [that had been] cleared of snow so that the children could ice-skate?

"We don't want to have to fence off the access, and we certainly don't want to go to war with the fishermen that come up for a good time and try to be considerate neighbors.

"We only ask that the fishermen be considerate of us. Please drive carefully for the sake of the small children who live here. Give us the same consideration that you would want us to give your families and your property in your neighborhood.

"Thank you for helping.

"The subdivision folks!"

Methods and magic, and a bit of manners, combine in the best of ice fishing.

We were embarrassed reading that letter back then, ashamed of fellow fishermen, and secretly afraid that maybe we'd blocked a driveway or cussed a little louder than necessary.

But setting the letter down on the seat of the car those years ago, out of the corner of my eye, I saw your kid Chuck, then just ten years old. The bluegill fishing had been slow, and he'd become a little bored. Instead of moping or causing trouble, in fifteen minutes he'd carefully gathered a handful of trash left by others. He'd carried it back to the car, and now, after hearing me read the letter aloud, smiled to himself as he looked at the litter.

I smiled, too. You turned, briefly, at my urging, and smiled also.

One of the best things about an ice angler's sunset, after all, just might be the promise it makes of an even better fishing day tomorrow.